50 Japanese Variation Recipes for Home

By: Kelly Johnson

Table of Contents

- Sushi Rolls with Avocado and Cucumber
- Teriyaki Chicken with Sesame Seeds
- Miso Soup with Tofu and Wakame
- Tempura Shrimp with Dipping Sauce
- Yakitori Skewers with Chicken and Scallions
- Udon Noodle Soup with Tempura Vegetables
- Tonkatsu Pork Cutlets with Cabbage Salad
- California Roll with Crab and Avocado
- Okonomiyaki Savory Pancakes with Bonito Flakes
- Gyoza Dumplings with Pork and Ginger
- Chirashi Sushi Bowl with Assorted Fish
- Matcha Green Tea Ice Cream
- Takoyaki Octopus Balls with Mayo and Soy Sauce
- Beef Sukiyaki Hot Pot with Vegetables
- Chicken Katsu Curry with Rice
- Inari Sushi Stuffed Tofu Pockets
- Soba Noodle Salad with Sesame Dressing
- Mochi Ice Cream Balls
- Pork Ramen with Soft-Boiled Egg
- Dynamite Roll with Spicy Tuna and Sriracha
- Hiyayakko Cold Tofu with Soy Sauce and Green Onions
- Nikujaga Beef and Potato Stew
- Anmitsu Jelly Dessert with Fruit and Red Bean Paste
- Shabu-Shabu Hot Pot with Thinly Sliced Beef
- Zaru Soba Cold Buckwheat Noodles with Dipping Sauce
- Tamago Sushi Rolled Omelette
- Chicken Teriyaki Donburi Rice Bowl
- Yaki Onigiri Grilled Rice Balls
- Chawanmushi Steamed Egg Custard
- Salmon Sashimi with Wasabi and Soy Sauce
- Katsudon Breaded Pork Cutlet Rice Bowl
- Unagi Don Grilled Eel Rice Bowl
- Tofu Dengaku Grilled Tofu with Miso Glaze
- Spicy Tuna Roll with Sriracha Mayo
- Yakisoba Stir-Fried Noodles with Pork and Vegetables

- Taiyaki Fish-Shaped Cake with Sweet Red Bean Filling
- Oyakodon Chicken and Egg Rice Bowl
- Zucchini and Carrot Sunomono Vinegar Salad
- Chicken Karaage Japanese Fried Chicken
- Horenso no Goma-ae Spinach with Sesame Dressing
- Red Bean Dorayaki Pancakes
- Chicken Yakisoba Stir-Fried Noodles
- Kappa Maki Cucumber Sushi Rolls
- Nasu Dengaku Miso-Glazed Eggplant
- Chuka Kurage Sunomono Jellyfish Salad
- Kakiage Mixed Vegetable Tempura
- Inarizushi Fried Tofu Pouch Sushi
- Sake Steamed Clams with Sake and Butter
- Edamame Boiled Soybeans with Sea Salt
- Chicken Nanban Fried Chicken with Tartar Sauce

Sushi Rolls with Avocado and Cucumber

Ingredients:

- 2 cups sushi rice
- 2 1/2 cups water
- 1/4 cup rice vinegar
- 2 tablespoons sugar
- 1 teaspoon salt
- 2 nori seaweed sheets
- 1 ripe avocado, thinly sliced
- 1 cucumber, julienned
- Soy sauce, for serving
- Pickled ginger, for serving
- Wasabi, for serving

Instructions:

1. Rinse the sushi rice under cold water until the water runs clear. Combine the rice and water in a rice cooker and cook according to the manufacturer's instructions.
2. In a small saucepan, heat the rice vinegar, sugar, and salt over low heat until the sugar and salt are dissolved. Remove from heat and let it cool.
3. Once the rice is cooked, transfer it to a large bowl and gently fold in the vinegar mixture using a wooden spoon or spatula. Be careful not to mash the rice.
4. Place a nori seaweed sheet shiny side down on a bamboo sushi mat or a clean kitchen towel.
5. With wet hands, spread a thin layer of sushi rice evenly over the nori, leaving a 1-inch border at the top.
6. Arrange the avocado and cucumber slices in a single layer along the bottom edge of the nori.
7. Starting from the bottom, tightly roll the sushi using the bamboo mat or kitchen towel, pressing gently as you roll to seal the edge.
8. Wet the top border of the nori with a little water to seal the roll.
9. Repeat the process with the remaining nori, rice, avocado, and cucumber.
10. Use a sharp knife to slice each roll into 6-8 pieces.
11. Serve the sushi rolls with soy sauce, pickled ginger, and wasabi on the side.

Enjoy your delicious Sushi Rolls with Avocado and Cucumber!

Teriyaki Chicken with Sesame Seeds

Ingredients:

- 2 boneless, skinless chicken breasts
- 1/4 cup soy sauce
- 2 tablespoons honey
- 2 tablespoons mirin (Japanese rice wine)
- 1 tablespoon rice vinegar
- 1 teaspoon sesame oil
- 2 cloves garlic, minced
- 1 teaspoon grated ginger
- 1 tablespoon sesame seeds
- 2 green onions, thinly sliced (optional)
- Cooked rice, for serving
- Steamed vegetables, for serving (optional)

Instructions:

1. Slice the chicken breasts into thin strips or bite-sized pieces.
2. In a bowl, whisk together the soy sauce, honey, mirin, rice vinegar, sesame oil, minced garlic, and grated ginger to make the teriyaki sauce.
3. Place the chicken pieces in a shallow dish or resealable plastic bag. Pour half of the teriyaki sauce over the chicken, reserving the other half for later. Toss the chicken to coat evenly in the sauce. Marinate in the refrigerator for at least 30 minutes, or up to 2 hours for maximum flavor.
4. Heat a skillet or frying pan over medium-high heat. Add the marinated chicken pieces and cook for 4-5 minutes on each side, or until cooked through and caramelized, brushing with the remaining teriyaki sauce halfway through cooking.
5. Sprinkle sesame seeds over the cooked chicken pieces and toss to coat evenly.
6. Transfer the teriyaki chicken to a serving plate and garnish with sliced green onions, if desired.
7. Serve hot with steamed rice and your choice of steamed vegetables.
8. Enjoy your delicious Teriyaki Chicken with Sesame Seeds!

This dish is perfect for a quick and flavorful meal at home.

Miso Soup with Tofu and Wakame

Ingredients:

- 4 cups water
- 3 tablespoons miso paste (white or red miso)
- 1/2 cup dried wakame seaweed
- 1/2 block tofu, diced into small cubes
- 2 green onions, thinly sliced
- 1 tablespoon soy sauce (optional)
- 1 teaspoon sesame oil (optional)

Instructions:

1. Start by soaking the dried wakame seaweed in cold water for about 5 minutes, or until it's rehydrated and soft. Drain the water and set the wakame aside.
2. In a pot, bring 4 cups of water to a simmer over medium heat.
3. Once the water is simmering, add the rehydrated wakame and diced tofu to the pot. Let them cook for about 2-3 minutes, or until the tofu is heated through.
4. In a small bowl, whisk together the miso paste with a few tablespoons of warm water until it's smooth and well combined.
5. Lower the heat of the pot to low, and then slowly pour the miso mixture into the soup, stirring gently to incorporate it.
6. Let the soup simmer for another 1-2 minutes, but do not let it boil, as boiling miso can cause it to lose its flavor.
7. Taste the soup and adjust the seasoning if necessary. You can add soy sauce for extra saltiness or sesame oil for additional flavor.
8. Finally, add thinly sliced green onions to the soup for freshness and color.
9. Once everything is well combined and heated through, remove the pot from the heat.
10. Serve the miso soup hot in bowls and enjoy its comforting warmth and rich umami flavor.

This Miso Soup with Tofu and Wakame makes for a comforting and nutritious meal, perfect for any time of the day.

Tempura Shrimp with Dipping Sauce

Ingredients:

For Tempura Shrimp:

- 10 large shrimp, peeled and deveined
- 1 cup all-purpose flour
- 1/2 cup cornstarch
- 1 teaspoon baking powder
- 1 cup ice-cold water
- Vegetable oil, for frying
- Salt, to taste

For Dipping Sauce:

- 1/4 cup soy sauce
- 2 tablespoons mirin (Japanese sweet rice wine)
- 1 tablespoon rice vinegar
- 1 teaspoon grated ginger
- 1 teaspoon grated daikon radish (optional)
- 1 green onion, thinly sliced (optional)

Instructions:

1. Start by preparing the dipping sauce. In a small bowl, combine the soy sauce, mirin, rice vinegar, grated ginger, and grated daikon radish. Stir well to combine. Set aside.
2. Prepare the shrimp by patting them dry with paper towels. Make a few shallow cuts along the inner curve of each shrimp to prevent them from curling up when frying. Season the shrimp lightly with salt.
3. In a large bowl, sift together the all-purpose flour, cornstarch, and baking powder. Gradually add the ice-cold water to the flour mixture, whisking gently until just combined. It's okay if there are still lumps in the batter.
4. Heat vegetable oil in a deep fryer or large pot to 350°F (175°C).
5. Dip each shrimp into the batter, ensuring it's evenly coated.

6. Carefully place the battered shrimp into the hot oil, one at a time, and fry in batches to avoid overcrowding the pot. Fry the shrimp for about 2-3 minutes, or until they are golden brown and crispy.
7. Once the shrimp are cooked, use a slotted spoon or wire mesh skimmer to remove them from the oil and transfer them to a plate lined with paper towels to drain excess oil.
8. Repeat the battering and frying process with the remaining shrimp.
9. Serve the tempura shrimp hot with the dipping sauce on the side. Garnish with thinly sliced green onions, if desired.

Enjoy your crispy Tempura Shrimp with Dipping Sauce as a delightful appetizer or main dish!

Yakitori Skewers with Chicken and Scallions

Ingredients:

For the Yakitori Sauce:

- 1/2 cup soy sauce
- 1/4 cup mirin (Japanese sweet rice wine)
- 1/4 cup sake (Japanese rice wine)
- 2 tablespoons granulated sugar
- 2 cloves garlic, minced
- 1 teaspoon grated ginger

For the Skewers:

- 1 lb (450g) boneless, skinless chicken thighs, cut into bite-sized pieces
- 6-8 scallions (green onions), cut into 1-inch pieces
- Bamboo skewers, soaked in water for at least 30 minutes

Instructions:

1. In a small saucepan, combine soy sauce, mirin, sake, sugar, minced garlic, and grated ginger to make the Yakitori sauce. Bring the mixture to a simmer over medium heat, stirring occasionally until the sugar is dissolved. Let it simmer for about 5-7 minutes until slightly thickened. Remove from heat and let it cool.
2. Preheat your grill or broiler to medium-high heat.
3. Thread the chicken pieces and scallion pieces alternately onto the soaked bamboo skewers.
4. Brush the skewers generously with the Yakitori sauce, reserving some sauce for basting while grilling.
5. Grill or broil the skewers for about 3-4 minutes on each side, or until the chicken is cooked through and the edges are slightly charred. Baste the skewers with the remaining Yakitori sauce while grilling.
6. Once the chicken is cooked through, remove the skewers from the grill or broiler and let them rest for a couple of minutes.
7. Serve the Yakitori skewers hot, garnished with extra chopped scallions if desired.

Enjoy your delicious Yakitori Skewers with Chicken and Scallions as a flavorful appetizer or main dish!

Udon Noodle Soup with Tempura Vegetables

Ingredients:

For Tempura Vegetables:

- 1 cup all-purpose flour
- 1/2 cup cornstarch
- 1 teaspoon baking powder
- 1 cup ice-cold water
- Assorted vegetables (such as sweet potatoes, zucchini, bell peppers, and broccoli), sliced into bite-sized pieces
- Vegetable oil, for frying
- Salt, to taste

For Udon Noodle Soup:

- 4 cups dashi stock (or vegetable broth for a vegetarian option)
- 2 tablespoons soy sauce
- 1 tablespoon mirin (Japanese sweet rice wine)
- 1 tablespoon sake (Japanese rice wine)
- 1 tablespoon sugar
- 2 packs (14 oz/400g each) fresh or dried udon noodles
- 2 green onions, thinly sliced
- Shichimi togarashi (Japanese seven spice blend), for garnish (optional)
- Nori (seaweed sheets), cut into thin strips, for garnish (optional)

Instructions:

1. Start by preparing the tempura batter. In a large bowl, sift together the all-purpose flour, cornstarch, and baking powder. Gradually add the ice-cold water to the flour mixture, whisking gently until just combined. It's okay if there are still lumps in the batter. Place the batter in the refrigerator to keep it cold while you prepare the vegetables and soup.
2. In a medium pot, combine dashi stock (or vegetable broth), soy sauce, mirin, sake, and sugar. Bring the mixture to a simmer over medium heat. Let it simmer

for about 5 minutes to allow the flavors to meld. Taste and adjust seasoning if necessary.
3. Cook the udon noodles according to the package instructions. If using fresh udon noodles, they usually cook in boiling water for about 1-2 minutes. If using dried udon noodles, cook them according to the package instructions, usually around 8-10 minutes. Drain the noodles and set aside.
4. Heat vegetable oil in a deep fryer or large pot to 350°F (175°C).
5. Dip the sliced vegetables into the tempura batter, ensuring they are evenly coated.
6. Carefully place the battered vegetables into the hot oil, one at a time, and fry in batches to avoid overcrowding the pot. Fry the vegetables for about 2-3 minutes, or until they are golden brown and crispy. Use a slotted spoon or wire mesh skimmer to remove them from the oil and transfer them to a plate lined with paper towels to drain excess oil.
7. Once all the vegetables are fried, divide the cooked udon noodles among serving bowls.
8. Ladle the hot udon noodle soup over the noodles in each bowl.
9. Top each bowl with a few pieces of tempura vegetables and garnish with thinly sliced green onions, shichimi togarashi, and nori strips, if desired.
10. Serve the Udon Noodle Soup with Tempura Vegetables hot and enjoy its comforting warmth and delightful flavors!

This dish makes for a satisfying and delicious meal, perfect for any time of the year.

Tonkatsu Pork Cutlets with Cabbage Salad

Ingredients:

For Tonkatsu Pork Cutlets:

- 4 boneless pork loin chops, about 1/2-inch thick
- Salt and pepper, to taste
- 1/2 cup all-purpose flour
- 2 large eggs, beaten
- 1 cup panko breadcrumbs
- Vegetable oil, for frying

For Cabbage Salad:

- 4 cups shredded cabbage
- 1 carrot, julienned
- 2 green onions, thinly sliced
- 2 tablespoons rice vinegar
- 1 tablespoon soy sauce
- 1 teaspoon sugar
- 1 teaspoon sesame oil
- Salt and pepper, to taste

For Tonkatsu Sauce (optional):

- 1/4 cup ketchup
- 2 tablespoons Worcestershire sauce
- 1 tablespoon soy sauce
- 1 tablespoon mirin (Japanese sweet rice wine)

Instructions:

1. Start by preparing the cabbage salad. In a large bowl, combine the shredded cabbage, julienned carrot, and thinly sliced green onions.
2. In a small bowl, whisk together the rice vinegar, soy sauce, sugar, sesame oil, salt, and pepper to make the dressing for the cabbage salad.
3. Pour the dressing over the cabbage mixture and toss until well combined. Set aside to marinate while you prepare the pork cutlets.
4. Place each pork loin chop between two sheets of plastic wrap or parchment paper. Use a meat mallet or rolling pin to pound the pork chops to an even thickness, about 1/4-inch thick. Season both sides of the pork chops with salt and pepper.
5. Set up a breading station with three shallow bowls. Place the all-purpose flour in the first bowl, beaten eggs in the second bowl, and panko breadcrumbs in the third bowl.
6. Dredge each pork chop in the flour, shaking off any excess. Dip the floured pork chop into the beaten eggs, allowing any excess to drip off. Finally, coat the pork chop evenly with panko breadcrumbs, pressing gently to adhere.
7. Heat vegetable oil in a large skillet or frying pan over medium-high heat. The oil should be hot enough to sizzle when a breadcrumb is added but not smoking.
8. Carefully place the breaded pork chops in the hot oil, working in batches if necessary to avoid overcrowding the pan. Fry the pork chops for about 3-4 minutes on each side, or until they are golden brown and crispy. Use tongs to flip the pork chops halfway through cooking.
9. Once the pork chops are cooked through and crispy, transfer them to a plate lined with paper towels to drain excess oil.
10. If making Tonkatsu sauce, combine ketchup, Worcestershire sauce, soy sauce, and mirin in a small bowl. Stir until well combined.
11. Serve the Tonkatsu Pork Cutlets hot alongside the cabbage salad. Drizzle Tonkatsu sauce over the pork cutlets if desired, or serve it on the side for dipping.
12. Enjoy your delicious Tonkatsu Pork Cutlets with Cabbage Salad!

This dish is a classic Japanese comfort food that's sure to satisfy your cravings.

California Roll with Crab and Avocado

Ingredients:

For Sushi Rice:

- 1 cup sushi rice
- 1 1/4 cups water
- 2 tablespoons rice vinegar
- 1 tablespoon sugar
- 1/2 teaspoon salt

For California Roll:

- 2 sheets nori (seaweed)
- 1/2 lb imitation crab meat, shredded
- 1 ripe avocado, thinly sliced
- 1/2 cucumber, julienned
- Toasted sesame seeds, for garnish (optional)
- Soy sauce, for serving
- Pickled ginger, for serving
- Wasabi, for serving

Instructions:

1. Rinse the sushi rice under cold water until the water runs clear. Combine the rice and water in a rice cooker and cook according to the manufacturer's instructions.
2. In a small saucepan, heat the rice vinegar, sugar, and salt over low heat until the sugar and salt are dissolved. Remove from heat and let it cool.
3. Once the rice is cooked, transfer it to a large bowl and gently fold in the vinegar mixture using a wooden spoon or spatula. Be careful not to mash the rice. Let the rice cool to room temperature.
4. Place a bamboo sushi mat or a clean kitchen towel on a flat surface. Lay a sheet of nori shiny side down on the mat or towel.
5. With wet hands, spread a thin layer of sushi rice evenly over the nori, leaving a 1-inch border at the top.

6. Arrange the shredded imitation crab meat, avocado slices, and julienned cucumber in a line across the center of the rice.
7. Starting from the bottom, tightly roll the sushi using the bamboo mat or kitchen towel, pressing gently as you roll to seal the edge.
8. Wet the top border of the nori with a little water to seal the roll.
9. Use a sharp knife to slice the roll into 6-8 pieces.
10. Repeat the process with the remaining nori, rice, crab, avocado, and cucumber.
11. Arrange the California Roll pieces on a serving platter and sprinkle toasted sesame seeds over the top for garnish, if desired.
12. Serve the California Roll with soy sauce, pickled ginger, and wasabi on the side.

Enjoy your homemade California Roll with Crab and Avocado as a delicious and satisfying sushi treat!

Okonomiyaki Savory Pancakes with Bonito Flakes

Ingredients:

For Okonomiyaki Batter:

- 1 cup all-purpose flour
- 1 cup dashi stock (or water)
- 2 eggs
- 1/2 teaspoon salt
- 2 cups shredded cabbage
- 1/2 cup sliced green onions
- 1/2 cup thinly sliced pork belly or bacon (optional)
- 1/4 cup pickled red ginger (beni shoga), chopped (optional)
- Vegetable oil, for frying

For Toppings and Sauce:

- Okonomiyaki sauce (store-bought or homemade)
- Japanese mayonnaise
- Aonori (dried green seaweed flakes)
- Katsuobushi (bonito flakes)
- Thinly sliced green onions

Instructions:

1. In a large bowl, whisk together the all-purpose flour, dashi stock (or water), eggs, and salt until smooth.
2. Add the shredded cabbage, sliced green onions, sliced pork belly or bacon (if using), and chopped pickled red ginger (if using) to the batter. Mix until everything is evenly coated.
3. Heat a non-stick skillet or griddle over medium heat and lightly grease it with vegetable oil.
4. Pour a ladleful of the okonomiyaki batter onto the skillet, spreading it out into a round pancake shape, about 1/2 inch thick.
5. Cook the okonomiyaki for 3-4 minutes on each side, or until golden brown and cooked through. Use a spatula to gently flip the okonomiyaki.

6. Once both sides are cooked and golden brown, transfer the okonomiyaki to a serving plate.
7. Drizzle okonomiyaki sauce and Japanese mayonnaise over the top of the okonomiyaki.
8. Sprinkle aonori (dried green seaweed flakes) and katsuobushi (bonito flakes) generously over the sauce.
9. Garnish with thinly sliced green onions.
10. Serve the okonomiyaki immediately while hot.

Enjoy your delicious Okonomiyaki Savory Pancakes with Bonito Flakes as a flavorful and satisfying Japanese treat!

Gyoza Dumplings with Pork and Ginger

Ingredients:

For the Filling:

- 1/2 lb ground pork
- 2 cups finely chopped cabbage
- 2 green onions, finely chopped
- 2 cloves garlic, minced
- 1 tablespoon ginger, grated
- 1 tablespoon soy sauce
- 1 tablespoon sesame oil
- 1 teaspoon sugar
- 1/2 teaspoon salt
- 1/4 teaspoon black pepper

For the Wrapper:

- 30 round gyoza wrappers
- Water (for sealing)

For Dipping Sauce:

- 1/4 cup soy sauce
- 2 tablespoons rice vinegar
- 1 teaspoon sesame oil
- 1 teaspoon sugar
- 1 clove garlic, minced (optional)
- 1 teaspoon ginger, grated (optional)
- Chili oil or Sriracha (optional, for heat)

Instructions:

1. In a large bowl, combine the ground pork, chopped cabbage, green onions, minced garlic, grated ginger, soy sauce, sesame oil, sugar, salt, and black pepper. Mix until well combined.
2. To assemble the gyoza dumplings, place a small spoonful of the filling in the center of a gyoza wrapper. Dip your finger in water and moisten the edge of the wrapper. Fold the wrapper in half over the filling to form a half-moon shape. Pinch the edges together to seal, pleating one side if desired. Repeat with the remaining wrappers and filling.
3. Heat a tablespoon of vegetable oil in a large skillet or non-stick pan over medium-high heat. Once hot, arrange the gyoza dumplings in the skillet in a single layer, making sure they are not touching each other. Cook for 2-3 minutes, or until the bottoms are golden brown.
4. Carefully add 1/4 cup of water to the skillet and immediately cover with a lid. Reduce the heat to medium-low and let the dumplings steam for 6-8 minutes, or until the wrappers are translucent and the filling is cooked through.
5. While the dumplings are cooking, prepare the dipping sauce. In a small bowl, combine soy sauce, rice vinegar, sesame oil, sugar, minced garlic (if using), grated ginger (if using), and chili oil or Sriracha (if using). Stir until the sugar is dissolved.
6. Once the dumplings are cooked, remove the lid and increase the heat to medium-high. Cook for another 1-2 minutes, or until the remaining water has evaporated and the bottoms of the dumplings are crispy.
7. Transfer the gyoza dumplings to a serving plate and serve hot with the dipping sauce on the side.

Enjoy your homemade Gyoza Dumplings with Pork and Ginger as a delicious appetizer or snack!

Chirashi Sushi Bowl with Assorted Fish

Ingredients:

For Sushi Rice:

- 2 cups sushi rice
- 2 1/2 cups water
- 1/4 cup rice vinegar
- 2 tablespoons sugar
- 1 teaspoon salt

For Assorted Fish:

- 8 oz sashimi-grade fish (such as tuna, salmon, yellowtail, or shrimp), thinly sliced
- 1 tablespoon soy sauce
- 1 teaspoon sesame oil
- 1 teaspoon grated ginger
- 1 teaspoon wasabi (optional)
- Assorted toppings: sliced cucumber, avocado, radish sprouts, shredded nori (seaweed), tobiko (flying fish roe), sesame seeds, etc.

Instructions:

1. Rinse the sushi rice under cold water until the water runs clear. Combine the rice and water in a rice cooker and cook according to the manufacturer's instructions.
2. In a small saucepan, heat the rice vinegar, sugar, and salt over low heat until the sugar and salt are dissolved. Remove from heat and let it cool.
3. Once the rice is cooked, transfer it to a large bowl and gently fold in the vinegar mixture using a wooden spoon or spatula. Be careful not to mash the rice. Let the rice cool to room temperature.
4. In a separate bowl, combine the thinly sliced fish with soy sauce, sesame oil, and grated ginger. Toss gently to coat the fish evenly. Set aside.
5. To assemble the Chirashi Sushi Bowl, divide the sushi rice among serving bowls.
6. Arrange the marinated fish slices, sliced cucumber, avocado, radish sprouts, shredded nori, tobiko, and any other desired toppings on top of the rice.

7. Optionally, serve with a small dollop of wasabi on the side.
8. Sprinkle sesame seeds over the top for garnish.
9. Serve the Chirashi Sushi Bowl immediately and enjoy!

This dish offers a beautiful presentation of assorted fish and toppings over seasoned sushi rice, providing a delightful balance of flavors and textures.

Matcha Green Tea Ice Cream

Ingredients:

- 2 cups heavy cream
- 1 cup whole milk
- 3/4 cup granulated sugar
- 3 tablespoons matcha green tea powder
- 4 large egg yolks
- 1 teaspoon vanilla extract

Instructions:

1. In a saucepan, combine the heavy cream, whole milk, and matcha green tea powder. Whisk together until the matcha powder is fully dissolved.
2. Place the saucepan over medium heat and bring the mixture to a gentle simmer, stirring occasionally. Remove from heat once it starts to steam, but before it comes to a boil.
3. In a separate bowl, whisk together the egg yolks and sugar until pale and creamy.
4. Slowly pour the hot matcha cream mixture into the egg yolk mixture, whisking constantly to temper the eggs.
5. Pour the combined mixture back into the saucepan and return it to the stovetop over medium heat.
6. Cook the mixture, stirring constantly, until it thickens slightly and coats the back of a spoon. This usually takes about 5-7 minutes. Be careful not to let it boil.
7. Once thickened, remove the mixture from heat and strain it through a fine mesh sieve into a clean bowl to remove any lumps.
8. Stir in the vanilla extract.
9. Cover the bowl with plastic wrap, pressing it directly onto the surface of the mixture to prevent a skin from forming. Chill the mixture in the refrigerator for at least 4 hours, or preferably overnight.
10. Once chilled, churn the mixture in an ice cream maker according to the manufacturer's instructions until it reaches a soft-serve consistency.
11. Transfer the churned ice cream to a freezer-safe container and freeze for an additional 4 hours, or until firm.
12. Serve the matcha green tea ice cream scooped into bowls or cones, and enjoy its creamy, slightly bitter-sweet flavor!

This homemade matcha green tea ice cream is a delightful treat for matcha lovers, perfect for enjoying on its own or alongside other desserts.

Takoyaki Octopus Balls with Mayo and Soy Sauce

Ingredients:

For Takoyaki Batter:

- 2 cups all-purpose flour
- 4 large eggs
- 3 cups dashi stock (or water)
- 1 tablespoon soy sauce
- 1 tablespoon mirin (Japanese sweet rice wine)
- 1 teaspoon salt
- 1/2 teaspoon baking powder
- 1/2 cup finely chopped cooked octopus (or substitute with cooked shrimp, crab, or other seafood)
- 1/2 cup finely chopped green onions
- Takoyaki sauce (store-bought or homemade)
- Japanese mayonnaise
- Aonori (dried green seaweed flakes)
- Katsuobushi (bonito flakes)

Instructions:

1. In a large bowl, whisk together the all-purpose flour, eggs, dashi stock (or water), soy sauce, mirin, salt, and baking powder until smooth.
2. Preheat a takoyaki pan over medium heat and lightly grease the molds with oil or cooking spray.
3. Once the pan is hot, pour the batter into each mold, filling them about three-quarters full.
4. Add a small piece of chopped octopus and some chopped green onions into each mold.
5. Allow the batter to cook for a few minutes until the edges start to set and become golden brown.
6. Use a takoyaki pick or skewer to carefully flip each ball over so the uncooked batter can cook on the other side.
7. Continue to rotate and flip the balls until they are evenly cooked and golden brown on all sides, forming a spherical shape.

8. Once the takoyaki balls are cooked through and golden brown, transfer them to a serving plate.
9. Drizzle takoyaki sauce and Japanese mayonnaise generously over the top of the takoyaki balls.
10. Sprinkle aonori (dried green seaweed flakes) and katsuobushi (bonito flakes) generously over the sauce.
11. Serve the takoyaki balls immediately while hot.

Enjoy your homemade Takoyaki Octopus Balls with Mayo and Soy Sauce as a delicious and satisfying Japanese street food snack!

Beef Sukiyaki Hot Pot with Vegetables

Ingredients:

For Sukiyaki Sauce:

- 1/2 cup soy sauce
- 1/4 cup mirin (Japanese sweet rice wine)
- 1/4 cup sake (Japanese rice wine)
- 2 tablespoons sugar
- 2 tablespoons dashi stock (or water)

For Hot Pot:

- 1 lb thinly sliced beef (such as ribeye or sirloin)
- Assorted vegetables (such as Napa cabbage, spinach, mushrooms, carrots, onions, and green onions), thinly sliced or cut into bite-sized pieces
- 1 package firm tofu, sliced
- 4-6 shiitake mushrooms, stems removed and sliced
- 1/2 cup shirataki noodles (optional)
- 1 tablespoon vegetable oil
- 4 cups dashi stock (or beef broth)
- Cooked Japanese rice, for serving
- Raw eggs, for dipping (optional)

Instructions:

1. In a small saucepan, combine the soy sauce, mirin, sake, sugar, and dashi stock (or water) to make the sukiyaki sauce. Heat the mixture over medium heat until the sugar is dissolved. Set aside.
2. Heat a tablespoon of vegetable oil in a large skillet or sukiyaki pan over medium-high heat.
3. Add the thinly sliced beef to the skillet and cook for 1-2 minutes until it starts to brown.
4. Pour the sukiyaki sauce over the beef in the skillet. Add the sliced shiitake mushrooms and cook for another minute.

5. Arrange the assorted vegetables, tofu slices, and shirataki noodles (if using) around the beef in the skillet.
6. Pour the dashi stock (or beef broth) into the skillet, covering the ingredients. Bring the broth to a simmer.
7. Allow the ingredients to simmer in the broth for 3-4 minutes, or until the vegetables are tender and the beef is cooked through.
8. Once cooked, serve the beef sukiyaki hot pot directly from the skillet at the table.
9. To eat, dip the cooked ingredients into raw beaten eggs (optional) before enjoying with a bowl of hot steamed Japanese rice.
10. Enjoy your delicious Beef Sukiyaki Hot Pot with Vegetables as a comforting and hearty meal!

Sukiyaki is traditionally enjoyed as a communal dish, so gather around the table with family and friends to savor this flavorful Japanese hot pot together.

Chicken Katsu Curry with Rice

Ingredients:

For Chicken Katsu:

- 4 boneless, skinless chicken breasts
- Salt and pepper, to taste
- 1/2 cup all-purpose flour
- 2 large eggs, beaten
- 1 cup panko breadcrumbs
- Vegetable oil, for frying

For Curry Sauce:

- 2 tablespoons vegetable oil
- 1 onion, finely chopped
- 2 cloves garlic, minced
- 2 carrots, diced
- 2 potatoes, diced
- 2 tablespoons curry powder
- 3 cups chicken or vegetable broth
- 2 tablespoons soy sauce
- 1 tablespoon honey or sugar
- Salt, to taste

For Serving:

- Cooked Japanese rice

Instructions:

1. Start by preparing the Chicken Katsu. Place the chicken breasts between two sheets of plastic wrap and use a meat mallet or rolling pin to pound them to an even thickness. Season both sides of the chicken breasts with salt and pepper.
2. Set up a breading station with three shallow bowls. Place the all-purpose flour in the first bowl, beaten eggs in the second bowl, and panko breadcrumbs in the third bowl.
3. Dredge each chicken breast in the flour, shaking off any excess. Dip the floured chicken breast into the beaten eggs, allowing any excess to drip off. Finally, coat the chicken breast evenly with panko breadcrumbs, pressing gently to adhere.
4. Heat vegetable oil in a large skillet or frying pan over medium-high heat. Once hot, add the breaded chicken breasts to the skillet and cook for 3-4 minutes on each side, or until golden brown and cooked through. Transfer the cooked chicken katsu to a plate lined with paper towels to drain excess oil.
5. In the same skillet, heat 2 tablespoons of vegetable oil over medium heat. Add the finely chopped onion and minced garlic, and cook until softened and fragrant, about 2-3 minutes.
6. Add the diced carrots and potatoes to the skillet, and cook for another 5 minutes, stirring occasionally.
7. Stir in the curry powder and cook for another minute until fragrant.
8. Pour in the chicken or vegetable broth, soy sauce, and honey or sugar. Bring the mixture to a simmer, then reduce the heat to low and let it simmer for about 15-20 minutes, or until the vegetables are tender and the curry sauce has thickened slightly. Season with salt to taste.
9. While the curry sauce is simmering, slice the cooked chicken katsu into strips.
10. Serve the Chicken Katsu Curry over cooked Japanese rice. Place the sliced chicken katsu on top of the rice and ladle the curry sauce and vegetables over the chicken.
11. Enjoy your delicious Chicken Katsu Curry with Rice, a comforting and flavorful Japanese dish!

Feel free to adjust the seasoning and spice level of the curry sauce according to your taste preferences.

Inari Sushi Stuffed Tofu Pockets

Ingredients:

For Inari Sushi Pockets:

- 1 cup sushi rice
- 2 cups water
- 6-8 inari age (fried tofu pockets)
- 1 tablespoon sugar
- 2 tablespoons rice vinegar
- 1/2 teaspoon salt

For Filling (Optional):

- Cooked sushi rice mixed with rice vinegar, sugar, and salt
- Assorted vegetables (such as cucumber, avocado, or carrot), thinly sliced
- Cooked shrimp, crab, or smoked salmon
- Pickled ginger (beni shoga)
- Sesame seeds
- Nori (seaweed) strips

Instructions:

1. Rinse the sushi rice under cold water until the water runs clear. Combine the rice and water in a rice cooker and cook according to the manufacturer's instructions.
2. In a small saucepan, combine the sugar, rice vinegar, and salt. Heat over low heat until the sugar and salt are dissolved. Remove from heat and let it cool.
3. Once the rice is cooked, transfer it to a large bowl and gently fold in the vinegar mixture using a wooden spoon or spatula. Be careful not to mash the rice. Let the rice cool to room temperature.
4. Carefully open each inari age (fried tofu pocket) to form a pocket. Be careful not to tear the pockets.
5. Stuff each tofu pocket with a spoonful of sushi rice, filling it about two-thirds full. You can also add optional fillings such as thinly sliced vegetables, cooked seafood, pickled ginger, sesame seeds, or nori strips.

6. Press the rice gently to compact it inside the tofu pocket, ensuring it fills the pocket evenly.
7. Once stuffed, fold the edges of the tofu pocket over the rice to enclose the filling, forming a neat rectangle or square shape.
8. Repeat the process with the remaining tofu pockets and filling ingredients.
9. Arrange the stuffed tofu pockets on a serving platter and garnish with additional sesame seeds or nori strips, if desired.
10. Serve the Inari Sushi Stuffed Tofu Pockets as a delightful appetizer or snack, and enjoy the unique combination of flavors and textures!

Inari sushi makes for a delicious and convenient dish that's perfect for parties, picnics, or as a light meal. Feel free to customize the fillings according to your preferences for a personalized touch.

Soba Noodle Salad with Sesame Dressing

Ingredients:

For Soba Noodle Salad:

- 8 oz (225g) soba noodles
- 1 cup shredded carrots
- 1 cup thinly sliced cucumber
- 1/2 cup thinly sliced red bell pepper
- 1/4 cup sliced green onions
- 1/4 cup chopped fresh cilantro or parsley
- 1/4 cup toasted sesame seeds
- Optional: cooked shrimp, chicken, or tofu for added protein

For Sesame Dressing:

- 1/4 cup soy sauce
- 2 tablespoons rice vinegar
- 2 tablespoons sesame oil
- 1 tablespoon honey or maple syrup
- 1 tablespoon grated ginger
- 2 cloves garlic, minced
- 1 tablespoon sesame seeds
- 1 tablespoon chopped green onions (optional)

Instructions:

1. Cook the soba noodles according to the package instructions. Drain and rinse under cold water to stop the cooking process and cool the noodles. Set aside.
2. In a large bowl, combine the shredded carrots, thinly sliced cucumber, sliced red bell pepper, sliced green onions, chopped cilantro or parsley, and toasted sesame seeds. Add the cooked and cooled soba noodles to the bowl.
3. In a separate small bowl, whisk together the soy sauce, rice vinegar, sesame oil, honey or maple syrup, grated ginger, minced garlic, sesame seeds, and chopped green onions (if using) to make the sesame dressing.

4. Pour the sesame dressing over the soba noodle salad and toss until everything is evenly coated.
5. If using, add cooked shrimp, chicken, or tofu to the salad for added protein and flavor.
6. Serve the Soba Noodle Salad with Sesame Dressing immediately, or refrigerate for a few hours to allow the flavors to meld before serving.
7. Enjoy your delicious and refreshing Soba Noodle Salad as a light and satisfying meal or side dish!

This salad is perfect for lunch, dinner, or as a side dish for barbecues and picnics. Feel free to customize the salad with your favorite vegetables or protein options for added variety and nutrition.

Mochi Ice Cream Balls

Ingredients:

- 1 cup mochiko (sweet rice flour)
- 1/4 cup granulated sugar
- 1 cup water
- Cornstarch, for dusting
- Ice cream of your choice, slightly softened (common flavors include vanilla, green tea, strawberry, mango, etc.)
- Optional: Food coloring or flavoring extracts for colored or flavored mochi

Instructions:

1. In a microwave-safe bowl, whisk together the mochiko and sugar until well combined.
2. Gradually add the water to the mochiko mixture, stirring until smooth.
3. Microwave the mixture on high for 1 minute. Remove from the microwave and stir well.
4. Return the mixture to the microwave and microwave for another 1-2 minutes, stirring every 30 seconds, until the mixture is thick and sticky.
5. Dust a clean work surface with cornstarch.
6. Transfer the hot mochi mixture to the cornstarch-dusted surface and let it cool slightly until it's cool enough to handle.
7. Divide the mochi dough into small portions, about the size of a ping pong ball.
8. Flatten each portion of mochi dough into a circle using your fingers or a rolling pin.
9. Place a small scoop of slightly softened ice cream in the center of each mochi circle.
10. Gather the edges of the mochi circle around the ice cream ball and pinch to seal, forming a smooth ball.
11. Roll the mochi ice cream ball in additional cornstarch to prevent sticking.
12. Repeat the process with the remaining mochi dough and ice cream until all the ice cream is used.
13. Place the mochi ice cream balls on a baking sheet lined with parchment paper and freeze until firm, about 1-2 hours.

14. Once frozen, the mochi ice cream balls are ready to serve. Enjoy your delicious homemade Mochi Ice Cream Balls as a refreshing and delightful treat!

You can store any leftover mochi ice cream balls in an airtight container in the freezer for future enjoyment. Experiment with different ice cream flavors and colors to create a variety of mochi ice cream options!

Pork Ramen with Soft-Boiled Egg

Ingredients:

For Pork:

- 1 lb pork belly or pork shoulder, thinly sliced
- 2 tablespoons soy sauce
- 1 tablespoon mirin
- 1 tablespoon sake
- 1 tablespoon brown sugar
- 1 teaspoon grated ginger
- 1 teaspoon sesame oil

For Soft-Boiled Eggs:

- 4 large eggs
- Water, for boiling

For Ramen Noodles and Toppings:

- 8 oz ramen noodles
- 4 cups chicken broth
- 2 cloves garlic, minced
- 1-inch piece of ginger, sliced
- 2 tablespoons soy sauce
- 2 tablespoons mirin
- 1 tablespoon sesame oil
- Salt and pepper, to taste
- Thinly sliced green onions
- Sliced bamboo shoots (menma)
- Nori (dried seaweed sheets), torn into small pieces
- Toasted sesame seeds
- Chili oil or Sriracha (optional, for heat)

Instructions:

1. Start by marinating the pork. In a bowl, combine the soy sauce, mirin, sake, brown sugar, grated ginger, and sesame oil. Add the thinly sliced pork and mix until well coated. Let it marinate for at least 30 minutes, or overnight in the refrigerator for deeper flavor.
2. While the pork is marinating, prepare the soft-boiled eggs. Bring a pot of water to a boil. Gently lower the eggs into the boiling water and cook for 6-7 minutes for a soft-boiled egg. Remove the eggs with a slotted spoon and transfer them to a bowl of ice water to stop the cooking process. Once cooled, carefully peel the eggs and set them aside.
3. In a separate large pot, bring the chicken broth to a simmer over medium heat. Add the minced garlic, sliced ginger, soy sauce, mirin, and sesame oil. Let the broth simmer for about 15-20 minutes to allow the flavors to meld. Season with salt and pepper to taste.
4. While the broth is simmering, cook the marinated pork. Heat a skillet or frying pan over medium-high heat. Add the pork slices and cook for 2-3 minutes on each side until browned and cooked through. Remove from heat and set aside.
5. Cook the ramen noodles according to the package instructions. Drain and rinse the noodles under cold water to stop the cooking process.
6. To assemble the ramen bowls, divide the cooked noodles among serving bowls. Ladle the hot broth over the noodles.
7. Top each bowl with slices of cooked pork, a soft-boiled egg cut in half, thinly sliced green onions, sliced bamboo shoots, torn nori pieces, and toasted sesame seeds.
8. Optionally, drizzle chili oil or Sriracha over the top for added heat.
9. Serve the Pork Ramen with Soft-Boiled Egg immediately and enjoy your delicious homemade ramen!

Dynamite Roll with Spicy Tuna and Sriracha

Ingredients:

For Spicy Tuna:

- 1/2 lb sushi-grade tuna, finely diced
- 2 tablespoons mayonnaise
- 1 tablespoon Sriracha sauce
- 1 teaspoon soy sauce
- 1 teaspoon sesame oil
- 1/2 teaspoon sugar
- 1/2 teaspoon rice vinegar

For Dynamite Sauce:

- 1/4 cup mayonnaise
- 1 tablespoon Sriracha sauce
- 1 teaspoon honey
- 1 teaspoon rice vinegar

For Roll:

- 4 sheets nori (seaweed)
- 2 cups sushi rice, prepared
- 1/2 cucumber, julienned
- 1 avocado, sliced
- Sesame seeds, for garnish

Instructions:

1. Start by preparing the spicy tuna. In a bowl, combine the finely diced tuna, mayonnaise, Sriracha sauce, soy sauce, sesame oil, sugar, and rice vinegar. Mix well until the tuna is evenly coated. Set aside.

2. Next, make the dynamite sauce. In another bowl, combine the mayonnaise, Sriracha sauce, honey, and rice vinegar. Stir until smooth and well combined. Set aside.
3. Lay a bamboo sushi mat on a flat surface and place a sheet of nori on top, shiny side down.
4. Moisten your hands with water and spread a thin layer of sushi rice evenly over the nori, leaving a 1-inch border at the top.
5. Arrange a portion of the spicy tuna mixture, cucumber strips, and avocado slices in a line across the center of the rice.
6. Drizzle some dynamite sauce over the filling ingredients.
7. Starting from the bottom, tightly roll the sushi using the bamboo mat, pressing gently as you roll to seal the edge.
8. Wet the top border of the nori with a little water to seal the roll.
9. Use a sharp knife to slice the roll into 6-8 pieces.
10. Repeat the process with the remaining nori, rice, spicy tuna mixture, cucumber, avocado, and dynamite sauce.
11. Arrange the Dynamite Roll pieces on a serving platter and sprinkle sesame seeds over the top for garnish.
12. Serve the Dynamite Roll with additional dynamite sauce and soy sauce for dipping, if desired.

Enjoy your homemade Dynamite Roll with Spicy Tuna and Sriracha as a delicious and satisfying sushi treat!

Hiyayakko Cold Tofu with Soy Sauce and Green Onions

Ingredients:

- 1 block (14-16 oz) silken or soft tofu
- 2 tablespoons soy sauce
- 1 tablespoon mirin (Japanese sweet rice wine)
- 1 tablespoon rice vinegar
- 1 green onion, finely chopped
- Grated ginger, for garnish (optional)
- Toasted sesame seeds, for garnish (optional)

Instructions:

1. Carefully remove the tofu from its package and drain any excess water.
2. Slice the tofu into individual serving pieces and arrange them on a serving plate.
3. In a small bowl, mix together the soy sauce, mirin, and rice vinegar to make the sauce.
4. Pour the sauce over the tofu slices, making sure to evenly coat each piece.
5. Sprinkle the finely chopped green onions over the tofu.
6. Optionally, garnish with a little grated ginger and toasted sesame seeds for extra flavor and presentation.
7. Serve the Hiyayakko immediately as a refreshing appetizer or side dish.

This simple yet flavorful dish is commonly enjoyed in Japan during hot summer months due to its cooling properties. It's light, healthy, and bursting with umami flavor from the soy sauce and green onions. Enjoy!

Nikujaga Beef and Potato Stew

Ingredients:

- 1 lb thinly sliced beef (such as beef chuck or ribeye)
- 4 medium potatoes, peeled and cut into bite-sized chunks
- 2 medium carrots, peeled and sliced
- 1 onion, thinly sliced
- 2 cups dashi stock (or beef broth)
- 1/4 cup soy sauce
- 1/4 cup mirin (Japanese sweet rice wine)
- 2 tablespoons sugar
- 1 tablespoon vegetable oil
- Salt and pepper, to taste
- Thinly sliced green onions, for garnish (optional)

Instructions:

1. Heat the vegetable oil in a large pot or Dutch oven over medium heat. Add the thinly sliced beef and cook until browned on all sides.
2. Add the sliced onions to the pot and cook until they become translucent.
3. Pour in the dashi stock (or beef broth), soy sauce, mirin, and sugar. Stir to combine.
4. Add the potato chunks and carrot slices to the pot. Bring the mixture to a boil, then reduce the heat to low. Cover and simmer for about 20-25 minutes, or until the potatoes and carrots are tender.
5. Once the vegetables are cooked through, taste the stew and adjust the seasoning with salt and pepper, if needed.
6. Serve the Nikujaga hot, garnished with thinly sliced green onions if desired.
7. Enjoy your delicious Nikujaga beef and potato stew as a comforting and satisfying meal!

Nikujaga is often served with steamed rice and a side of pickles for a complete Japanese meal. It's a hearty dish that's perfect for warming you up on a chilly day.

Anmitsu Jelly Dessert with Fruit and Red Bean Paste

Ingredients:

For Anmitsu Jelly:

- 1 pack (10g) agar agar powder
- 4 cups water
- 1/2 cup sugar

For Serving:

- Canned fruit cocktail, drained
- Fresh fruits (such as strawberries, kiwi, oranges), sliced
- Sweetened red bean paste (anko)
- Kuromitsu (Japanese brown sugar syrup), for drizzling
- Shiro-an (sweet white bean paste) or ice cream (optional)
- Shiratama dango (rice flour dumplings) or mochi (optional)

Instructions:

1. In a saucepan, combine the agar agar powder and water. Let it sit for about 5 minutes to allow the agar agar to soften.
2. Place the saucepan over medium heat and bring the mixture to a boil, stirring occasionally.
3. Once boiling, reduce the heat to low and simmer for 2-3 minutes, stirring constantly until the agar agar is completely dissolved.
4. Add the sugar to the mixture and stir until dissolved. Remove the saucepan from heat.
5. Pour the agar agar mixture into a shallow dish or mold. Let it cool to room temperature, then refrigerate until set, about 1-2 hours.
6. Once the agar agar jelly is set, cut it into cubes or desired shapes.
7. To assemble the Anmitsu, divide the agar agar jelly cubes among serving bowls.
8. Add a spoonful of sweetened red bean paste (anko) to each bowl.
9. Arrange the drained canned fruit cocktail and sliced fresh fruits over the jelly cubes and red bean paste.

10. Drizzle some kuromitsu (Japanese brown sugar syrup) over the fruits and jelly.
11. Optionally, add a dollop of shiro-an (sweet white bean paste) or a scoop of ice cream on top of the fruits.
12. If desired, serve with shiratama dango (rice flour dumplings) or mochi on the side.
13. Enjoy your delicious Anmitsu jelly dessert with fruit and red bean paste as a refreshing and sweet treat!

Anmitsu is a delightful and customizable dessert that's perfect for any occasion. Feel free to adjust the toppings and additions according to your preference.

Shabu-Shabu Hot Pot with Thinly Sliced Beef

Ingredients:

For Broth:

- 6 cups dashi stock (or water)
- 2-inch piece of kombu (dried kelp)
- 1/4 cup sake (Japanese rice wine)
- 1/4 cup mirin (Japanese sweet rice wine)
- 1/4 cup soy sauce
- 2 tablespoons sugar
- Salt, to taste

For Hot Pot:

- 1 lb thinly sliced beef (such as ribeye or sirloin)
- Assorted vegetables (such as Napa cabbage, spinach, mushrooms, carrots, and green onions), thinly sliced or cut into bite-sized pieces
- Tofu, sliced
- Shirataki noodles (optional)
- Udon noodles (optional)
- Cooked rice, for serving
- Dipping sauces (such as ponzu sauce, sesame sauce, or goma dare)
- Condiments (such as grated daikon radish, chopped green onions, or grated ginger)

Instructions:

1. Start by preparing the broth. In a large pot, combine the dashi stock (or water) and kombu. Bring to a gentle simmer over medium heat and let it steep for about 10-15 minutes to infuse the flavors.
2. Remove the kombu from the pot and discard. Add the sake, mirin, soy sauce, and sugar to the broth. Stir well to combine.
3. Taste the broth and adjust the seasoning with salt if needed. Keep the broth warm over low heat while preparing the other ingredients.

4. Arrange the thinly sliced beef, assorted vegetables, tofu, and any other desired ingredients on serving plates or trays.
5. Set up a portable gas burner or electric hot pot on the dining table. Place the pot of broth on the burner and bring it to a simmer.
6. Each diner can then use chopsticks or a slotted spoon to cook their desired ingredients in the simmering broth. Dip the cooked ingredients into the dipping sauces or enjoy them with condiments.
7. Cook the beef slices briefly in the broth until they change color and are just cooked through. This process is called "shabu-shabu," where you swish the meat back and forth in the hot broth until cooked to your liking.
8. Add the assorted vegetables, tofu, and noodles to the hot pot and cook until tender.
9. Serve the cooked ingredients with steamed rice and enjoy your delicious Shabu-Shabu Hot Pot with Thinly Sliced Beef!

Shabu-Shabu is a fun and interactive dining experience that's perfect for gatherings with family and friends. Adjust the ingredients and dipping sauces according to your preferences for a personalized hot pot feast.

Zaru Soba Cold Buckwheat Noodles with Dipping Sauce

Ingredients:

- 200g soba noodles (dried buckwheat noodles)
- 3 cups of water for boiling
- Ice water (for chilling noodles)
- Dipping Sauce:
    - 1/2 cup soy sauce
    - 1/2 cup dashi (Japanese soup stock)
    - 1/4 cup mirin (sweet rice wine)
    - 1 tablespoon sugar
    - 1 green onion, finely chopped (optional)
    - Wasabi paste (optional, for serving)
- Toppings (optional, choose as per your preference):
    - Nori (seaweed), shredded
    - Shredded daikon radish
    - Shredded cucumber
    - Sliced green onions
    - Toasted sesame seeds

Instructions:

1. Cook the Soba Noodles:
    - Bring a large pot of water to a boil.
    - Add soba noodles to the boiling water and cook according to package instructions (usually about 4-5 minutes), stirring occasionally to prevent sticking.
    - Once cooked, drain the noodles and rinse under cold water to remove excess starch and stop the cooking process.
    - Transfer the noodles to a bowl of ice water to chill. This helps them to retain their texture and prevents them from sticking together.
2. Make the Dipping Sauce:
    - In a small saucepan, combine soy sauce, dashi, mirin, and sugar.
    - Heat the mixture over medium heat until the sugar dissolves, stirring occasionally.
    - Once the sugar has dissolved, remove the sauce from heat and let it cool to room temperature.

- Optionally, add finely chopped green onions to the sauce for extra flavor.
3. Prepare Toppings (Optional):
    - While the noodles and sauce are cooling, prepare any toppings you'd like to serve with your zaru soba. This can include shredded nori, daikon radish, cucumber, sliced green onions, or toasted sesame seeds. Arrange them on a plate for easy access.
4. Serve:
    - Once the noodles are chilled, drain them from the ice water and divide them among individual serving plates or bowls.
    - Serve the noodles with the dipping sauce in small bowls alongside the toppings.
    - Optionally, serve wasabi paste on the side for those who enjoy a bit of heat with their soba noodles.
5. Enjoy:
    - To eat, take a small portion of noodles with your chopsticks and dip them into the sauce. Add toppings according to your preference.
    - Savor the refreshing taste of the cold noodles and the umami-rich flavor of the dipping sauce.

Zaru soba is a versatile dish, so feel free to customize it with your favorite toppings or adjust the dipping sauce to suit your taste preferences. Enjoy your meal!

Tamago Sushi Rolled Omelette

Ingredients:

- 2 large eggs
- 2 tablespoons sugar
- 1 tablespoon mirin (sweet rice wine)
- 1 tablespoon soy sauce
- 1/2 tablespoon vegetable oil
- Sushi rice (cooked sushi rice seasoned with rice vinegar, sugar, and salt)
- Nori (optional, for wrapping)

Instructions:

1. Prepare the Sweet Omelette (Tamago):
    - In a bowl, whisk together eggs, sugar, mirin, and soy sauce until well combined and the sugar is dissolved.
    - Heat a non-stick frying pan over medium-low heat and lightly oil the surface with vegetable oil.
    - Pour a thin layer of the egg mixture into the pan, tilting the pan to spread it evenly.
    - Once the bottom is set but the top is still slightly runny, gently roll the omelette from one end of the pan to the other using a spatula or chopsticks.
    - Push the rolled omelette to one end of the pan and oil the empty space.
    - Pour another thin layer of the egg mixture into the pan, lifting the rolled omelette slightly to allow the new layer to flow underneath.
    - Once the new layer is partially set, roll it up again over the existing omelette.
    - Repeat this process until all of the egg mixture is used, rolling the omelette into a tight log shape.
    - Remove the rolled omelette from the pan and let it cool to room temperature.
2. Slice the Tamago:
    - Once cooled, slice the rolled omelette into thin, even slices. Each slice should be about the width of your sushi rice.
3. Prepare the Sushi Rice:

- If you haven't already, prepare sushi rice by cooking short-grain rice according to package instructions and seasoning it with rice vinegar, sugar, and salt. Let it cool to room temperature before using.
4. Assemble the Tamago Sushi:
    - Take a small amount of sushi rice and shape it into a small rectangular block using slightly wet hands.
    - Place a slice of tamago over the rice block. If desired, wrap a strip of nori around the sides of the rice and tamago to hold them together.
    - Repeat the process to make additional tamago sushi pieces.
5. Serve and Enjoy:
    - Arrange the tamago sushi pieces on a serving plate.
    - Serve with soy sauce, pickled ginger, and wasabi on the side, if desired.
    - Enjoy your homemade tamago sushi as a delightful snack or part of a sushi meal!

Tamago sushi is not only delicious but also visually appealing with its vibrant colors and layers. It's a great option for sushi lovers of all ages.

Chicken Teriyaki Donburi Rice Bowl

Ingredients:

- 2 boneless, skinless chicken breasts (or thighs), sliced into bite-sized pieces
- 2 tablespoons soy sauce
- 2 tablespoons mirin (sweet rice wine)
- 2 tablespoons sake (Japanese rice wine) or dry sherry
- 2 tablespoons sugar
- 1 tablespoon vegetable oil
- Cooked Japanese rice (short-grain or sushi rice)
- Steamed vegetables (such as broccoli, carrots, or snap peas), optional, for serving
- Sesame seeds, for garnish
- Sliced green onions, for garnish

Instructions:

1. Marinate the Chicken:
    - In a bowl, mix together soy sauce, mirin, sake (or sherry), and sugar until the sugar is dissolved.
    - Add the chicken pieces to the marinade, ensuring they are well coated. Let them marinate for at least 15-30 minutes in the refrigerator.
2. Cook the Chicken:
    - Heat vegetable oil in a large skillet or frying pan over medium-high heat.
    - Remove the chicken from the marinade, reserving the marinade for later use.
    - Add the chicken pieces to the hot skillet and cook until browned and cooked through, about 5-7 minutes, stirring occasionally.
    - Once the chicken is cooked, add the reserved marinade to the skillet. Bring to a simmer and cook for an additional 2-3 minutes, or until the sauce thickens and coats the chicken evenly.
3. Assemble the Donburi Bowls:
    - Divide the cooked rice among serving bowls.
    - Spoon the chicken teriyaki over the rice, ensuring each bowl gets an equal amount of chicken and sauce.
    - If desired, add steamed vegetables to the bowls alongside the chicken teriyaki.
4. Garnish and Serve:

- Garnish the Chicken Teriyaki Donburi bowls with sesame seeds and sliced green onions for added flavor and presentation.
- Serve immediately and enjoy the delicious combination of tender chicken, savory teriyaki sauce, and fluffy rice!

Chicken Teriyaki Donburi is a satisfying and comforting meal that can be enjoyed any day of the week. Feel free to customize it with your favorite vegetables or add a sprinkle of furikake (Japanese seasoning) for extra flavor.

Yaki Onigiri Grilled Rice Balls

Ingredients:

- Cooked Japanese rice (short-grain or sushi rice)
- Salt, to taste
- Vegetable oil, for grilling
- Optional toppings:
    - Soy sauce
    - Nori (seaweed), cut into strips
    - Furikake (Japanese seasoning)
    - Sesame seeds
    - Grilled meats or vegetables (such as teriyaki chicken, grilled mushrooms, or grilled salmon)

Instructions:

1. Prepare the Rice Balls:
    - Allow the cooked rice to cool slightly so it's easier to handle.
    - Moisten your hands with water to prevent the rice from sticking, then take a handful of rice and shape it into a compact ball. You can make them traditional round shape or triangular (oniigiri).
    - If desired, you can stuff the rice balls with fillings like umeboshi (pickled plum), cooked salmon, or grilled eel.
2. Season the Rice Balls:
    - Lightly sprinkle salt over the rice balls, coating them evenly. You can also season them with furikake or sesame seeds for extra flavor.
3. Grill the Rice Balls:
    - Heat a grill or a non-stick frying pan over medium heat. Brush the surface with vegetable oil to prevent sticking.
    - Place the rice balls on the grill or in the pan and cook for about 3-5 minutes on each side, or until they are golden brown and crispy on the outside.
    - If using a grill, you can achieve attractive grill marks by rotating the rice balls halfway through cooking.
4. Optional Toppings:
    - Once the rice balls are grilled to perfection, you can brush them with soy sauce for added flavor.

- Wrap nori strips around the rice balls to create a decorative and tasty outer layer.
5. Serve and Enjoy:
    - Transfer the grilled rice balls to a serving plate or a bento box.
    - Serve them hot as a snack or as part of a meal, alongside your favorite dipping sauce or grilled meats and vegetables.
    - Enjoy the crispy exterior and fluffy interior of these delicious yaki onigiri!

Yaki onigiri are versatile and can be enjoyed on their own or paired with various toppings and fillings. Get creative with your flavor combinations and enjoy the deliciousness of grilled rice balls!

Chawanmushi Steamed Egg Custard

Ingredients:

- 2 cups dashi (Japanese broth)
- 4 large eggs
- 1 tablespoon soy sauce
- 1 tablespoon mirin (sweet rice wine)
- Salt, to taste
- Optional ingredients (choose as per preference):
    - Cooked chicken slices
    - Cooked shrimp
    - Shiitake mushrooms, thinly sliced
    - Ginkgo nuts
    - Bamboo shoots
    - Kamaboko (fish cake), thinly sliced
    - Green peas
    - Mitsuba (Japanese parsley) or thinly sliced green onions, for garnish

Instructions:

1. Prepare the Dashi:
    - If you're using instant dashi granules, follow the package instructions to dissolve them in water and prepare the dashi. Alternatively, you can make dashi from scratch using kombu (dried kelp) and katsuobushi (dried bonito flakes).
2. Prepare the Custard Mixture:
    - In a mixing bowl, lightly beat the eggs.
    - Slowly pour the dashi into the beaten eggs while continuously whisking to combine.
    - Add soy sauce, mirin, and a pinch of salt to the mixture, and whisk until well incorporated.
3. Prepare the Ingredients:
    - Prepare your chosen ingredients by cooking them separately if they are not already cooked. For example, steam or boil chicken slices, shrimp, and any vegetables until they are just tender.
4. Assemble the Chawanmushi:

- Divide the cooked ingredients evenly among small cups or bowls. Ensure they cover the bottom of each cup or bowl.
- Gently pour the egg custard mixture over the ingredients in each cup, filling them almost to the top.

5. Steam the Chawanmushi:
   - Prepare a steamer and bring the water to a gentle simmer.
   - Carefully place the cups or bowls of chawanmushi into the steamer basket.
   - Cover the steamer and steam the chawanmushi over medium-low heat for about 15-20 minutes, or until the custard is set but still slightly jiggly in the center.
6. Serve and Enjoy:
   - Once the chawanmushi is cooked, carefully remove it from the steamer.
   - Garnish each cup or bowl with mitsuba or thinly sliced green onions for a pop of color.
   - Serve the chawanmushi hot as an appetizer or part of a Japanese meal.
   - Enjoy the silky-smooth texture and rich flavor of this comforting and elegant egg custard dish!

Chawanmushi is a versatile dish, so feel free to customize it with your favorite ingredients and adjust the seasonings to your taste preferences.

Salmon Sashimi with Wasabi and Soy Sauce

Ingredients:

- Fresh salmon fillet, sushi-grade
- Wasabi paste
- Soy sauce
- Optional garnishes:
    - Pickled ginger (gari)
    - Sliced cucumber
    - Shiso leaves
    - Toasted sesame seeds
    - Thinly sliced green onions

Instructions:

1. Prepare the Salmon:
    - Start with a fresh salmon fillet that has been properly handled and stored to ensure safety for raw consumption. It's essential to use sushi-grade salmon for sashimi.
    - Using a sharp knife, carefully slice the salmon against the grain into thin slices. Aim for slices that are about 1/4 to 1/2 inch thick. The slices should be uniform in size for even presentation.
2. Arrange the Sashimi:
    - Arrange the salmon slices neatly on a serving plate. You can overlap them slightly or fan them out for an elegant presentation.
    - If desired, you can place a small mound of grated daikon radish on the plate as a base for the salmon slices. This adds a refreshing crunch and helps to balance the flavors.
3. Serve with Wasabi and Soy Sauce:
    - Place a small dollop of wasabi paste on the side of the plate. Wasabi should be used sparingly, as it is very potent. You can adjust the amount according to your preference for heat.
    - Pour some soy sauce into a small dipping dish or bowl. Use low-sodium soy sauce if you prefer a milder flavor.
    - Optionally, you can mix a small amount of wasabi into the soy sauce to create a dipping sauce with extra kick.
4. Garnish (Optional):

- Garnish the salmon sashimi with thinly sliced green onions, toasted sesame seeds, or shiso leaves for added flavor and visual appeal.
- Serve pickled ginger (gari) on the side as a palate cleanser between bites.

5. Enjoy:
    - To eat, take a slice of salmon with your chopsticks or fingers and dip it lightly into the soy sauce and wasabi mixture. Be mindful not to overpower the delicate flavor of the salmon.
    - Enjoy the buttery texture and subtle flavor of the salmon sashimi with the kick of wasabi and the salty-sweetness of the soy sauce.

Salmon sashimi with wasabi and soy sauce makes for a light and refreshing appetizer or part of a Japanese-inspired meal. Make sure to use the freshest ingredients available for the best flavor and quality.

Katsudon Breaded Pork Cutlet Rice Bowl

Ingredients:

- 4 boneless pork loin chops (about 1/2-inch thick)
- Salt and pepper, to taste
- 1/2 cup all-purpose flour
- 2 large eggs, beaten
- 1 cup panko breadcrumbs
- Vegetable oil, for frying
- 4 cups cooked Japanese rice (short-grain or sushi rice)
- 4 large eggs, lightly beaten
- 2 cups dashi (Japanese broth) or chicken broth
- 4 tablespoons soy sauce
- 2 tablespoons mirin (sweet rice wine)
- 2 tablespoons sugar
- 1 onion, thinly sliced
- Sliced green onions, for garnish
- Pickled ginger (optional), for serving

Instructions:

1. Prepare the Pork Cutlets (Tonkatsu):
    - Season the pork chops with salt and pepper on both sides.
    - Set up a breading station with three shallow bowls: one with flour, one with beaten eggs, and one with panko breadcrumbs.
    - Dredge each pork chop in the flour, then dip into the beaten eggs, and coat evenly with panko breadcrumbs, pressing gently to adhere.
    - Heat vegetable oil in a large skillet over medium heat. Fry the breaded pork chops for about 3-4 minutes on each side, or until golden brown and cooked through. Drain on paper towels and set aside.
2. Make the Sauce:
    - In a separate saucepan, combine dashi (or chicken broth), soy sauce, mirin, and sugar. Bring to a simmer over medium heat.
    - Add the sliced onion to the simmering sauce and cook for about 5 minutes, or until the onions are softened.
3. Assemble the Katsudon:
    - Slice the fried pork cutlets into strips.
    - Divide the cooked rice among four serving bowls.

- Arrange the sliced pork cutlets on top of the rice in each bowl.
- Pour the beaten eggs evenly over the pork and rice in each bowl.
4. Cook the Eggs:
   - Place a lid on each bowl and cook over low heat for about 5 minutes, or until the eggs are just set.
5. Serve:
   - Remove the lids from the bowls.
   - Ladle the simmering onion and sauce mixture over each bowl of katsudon.
   - Garnish with sliced green onions and serve immediately, with pickled ginger on the side if desired.

Enjoy the comforting and satisfying flavors of katsudon, with crispy tonkatsu, fluffy rice, and savory-sweet sauce, all topped with creamy eggs. It's a popular dish in Japanese cuisine and perfect for a hearty meal!

Unagi Don Grilled Eel Rice Bowl

Ingredients:

- 2 unagi (freshwater eel) fillets, deboned
- 2 cups cooked Japanese rice (short-grain or sushi rice)
- 1/4 cup soy sauce
- 1/4 cup mirin (sweet rice wine)
- 2 tablespoons sugar
- 1 tablespoon sake (Japanese rice wine)
- 1 teaspoon grated ginger
- Optional toppings:
    - Toasted sesame seeds
    - Sliced green onions
    - Pickled ginger (gari)

Instructions:

1. Prepare the Eel:
    - If the unagi fillets are not pre-cooked, grill or broil them until cooked through. Alternatively, you can use pre-cooked unagi fillets that are available in many Asian grocery stores.
    - Once cooked, cut the eel fillets into smaller pieces for easier serving on top of the rice.
2. Make the Sauce:
    - In a small saucepan, combine soy sauce, mirin, sugar, sake, and grated ginger.
    - Heat the mixture over medium heat until the sugar dissolves, stirring occasionally.
    - Let the sauce simmer for a few minutes until it thickens slightly to form a glaze. Remove from heat.
3. Glaze the Eel:
    - Brush the cooked eel fillets generously with the prepared sauce, coating them evenly. Reserve some sauce for serving.
4. Assemble the Unagi Don:
    - Divide the cooked rice among serving bowls.
    - Place the glazed eel pieces on top of the rice in each bowl.
5. Serve:

- Drizzle a little more of the sauce over the eel and rice in each bowl.
- Optionally, sprinkle toasted sesame seeds and sliced green onions over the top for added flavor and garnish.
- Serve the Unagi Don hot, accompanied by pickled ginger (gari) on the side if desired.

Enjoy the rich and savory flavors of Unagi Don, where the tender, sweet eel pairs perfectly with the fluffy rice and aromatic sauce. It's a delightful dish that's sure to impress!

Tofu Dengaku Grilled Tofu with Miso Glaze

Ingredients:

- 1 block of firm tofu
- 2 tablespoons white miso paste
- 1 tablespoon mirin (sweet rice wine)
- 1 tablespoon sugar
- 1 tablespoon soy sauce
- Optional garnish:
    - Toasted sesame seeds
    - Thinly sliced green onions
    - Shichimi togarashi (Japanese seven spice blend)

Instructions:

1. Prepare the Tofu:
    - Drain the tofu and wrap it in a clean kitchen towel or paper towels. Place a heavy object on top of the wrapped tofu to press out excess water. Let it press for about 15-30 minutes to firm up the tofu.
2. Slice the Tofu:
    - Once the tofu is pressed, slice it into thick slices or cubes, depending on your preference.
3. Make the Miso Glaze:
    - In a small saucepan, combine white miso paste, mirin, sugar, and soy sauce.
    - Heat the mixture over medium heat, stirring continuously until the sugar is dissolved and the mixture is smooth. Remove from heat.
4. Grill or Broil the Tofu:
    - Preheat your grill or broiler to medium-high heat.
    - If grilling, lightly oil the grill grates. If broiling, line a baking sheet with parchment paper.
    - Place the tofu slices or cubes on the grill or baking sheet and cook for about 3-4 minutes on each side, or until lightly browned and grill marks appear.
5. Glaze the Tofu:
    - Brush the grilled tofu with the prepared miso glaze, coating each piece evenly.

- Return the glazed tofu to the grill or broiler and cook for an additional 1-2 minutes on each side, allowing the glaze to caramelize slightly.

6. Serve:
    - Transfer the glazed tofu to a serving plate.
    - Sprinkle toasted sesame seeds and thinly sliced green onions over the top for garnish, if desired.
    - Optionally, sprinkle with shichimi togarashi for added flavor and heat.
    - Serve the Tofu Dengaku hot as an appetizer or part of a Japanese-inspired meal.

Enjoy the deliciously savory and sweet flavors of Tofu Dengaku, where the tender tofu is complemented perfectly by the rich miso glaze. It's a delightful dish that's both satisfying and full of umami goodness!

Spicy Tuna Roll with Sriracha Mayo

Ingredients:

- 1 cup sushi rice (short-grain or sushi rice), cooked and seasoned
- 2-3 ounces sushi-grade tuna, finely chopped
- 1-2 teaspoons Sriracha sauce (adjust to taste)
- 1 tablespoon mayonnaise
- 1/2 teaspoon sesame oil
- 1/2 teaspoon soy sauce
- Nori sheets (seaweed)
- Bamboo sushi rolling mat
- Toasted sesame seeds (optional), for garnish
- Thinly sliced green onions (optional), for garnish

Instructions:

1. Prepare the Spicy Tuna Filling:
   - In a bowl, combine the finely chopped sushi-grade tuna, Sriracha sauce, mayonnaise, sesame oil, and soy sauce. Adjust the amount of Sriracha sauce to achieve your desired level of spiciness.
   - Mix the ingredients until well combined. The mixture should be creamy and evenly coated.
2. Assemble the Spicy Tuna Rolls:
   - Place a sheet of nori shiny side down on the bamboo sushi rolling mat.
   - With wet hands, spread a thin layer of seasoned sushi rice evenly over the nori, leaving about 1 inch of space at the top edge.
   - Spread a line of the spicy tuna mixture horizontally across the center of the rice-covered nori sheet.
   - Roll the sushi tightly using the bamboo mat, starting from the bottom edge, and apply gentle pressure to seal the roll.
3. Slice the Rolls:
   - Use a sharp, wet knife to slice the roll into individual pieces, about 1 inch thick. Wipe the knife clean between slices to ensure clean cuts.
4. Garnish and Serve:
   - Arrange the sliced Spicy Tuna Rolls on a serving plate.
   - Garnish with toasted sesame seeds and thinly sliced green onions, if desired, for added flavor and presentation.

- Serve the Spicy Tuna Rolls with additional soy sauce, pickled ginger, and wasabi on the side for dipping.
5. Enjoy:
    - Enjoy the Spicy Tuna Rolls with Sriracha Mayo as a delicious appetizer or part of a sushi feast at home!

These Spicy Tuna Rolls are easy to make and perfect for sushi lovers who enjoy a kick of heat. Adjust the spice level to your preference and have fun creating your own sushi rolls!

Yakisoba Stir-Fried Noodles with Pork and Vegetables

Ingredients:

- 200g yakisoba noodles (or substitute with ramen noodles or spaghetti)
- 150g thinly sliced pork belly or pork loin
- 1 small onion, thinly sliced
- 1 small carrot, julienned
- 1 small bell pepper (any color), thinly sliced
- 1 cup shredded cabbage
- 2 tablespoons vegetable oil
- 2 cloves garlic, minced
- 2 tablespoons soy sauce
- 1 tablespoon oyster sauce
- 1 tablespoon Worcestershire sauce
- 1 tablespoon ketchup
- 1 teaspoon sugar
- Salt and pepper, to taste
- Toasted sesame seeds, for garnish (optional)
- Thinly sliced green onions, for garnish (optional)

Instructions:

1. Prepare the Yakisoba Noodles:
    - If using dried yakisoba noodles, cook them according to the package instructions until al dente. Rinse under cold water to stop the cooking process and drain well. If using fresh yakisoba noodles, follow the package instructions.
2. Prepare the Sauce:
    - In a small bowl, mix together soy sauce, oyster sauce, Worcestershire sauce, ketchup, and sugar until well combined. Set aside.
3. Stir-Fry the Pork and Vegetables:
    - Heat 1 tablespoon of vegetable oil in a large skillet or wok over medium-high heat.
    - Add the sliced pork to the skillet and cook until it is no longer pink and slightly browned. Remove the pork from the skillet and set aside.
    - In the same skillet, add the remaining tablespoon of vegetable oil. Add the minced garlic and stir-fry for about 30 seconds, or until fragrant.

- Add the sliced onion, julienned carrot, and sliced bell pepper to the skillet. Stir-fry for 2-3 minutes, or until the vegetables are slightly softened.
- Add the shredded cabbage to the skillet and continue to stir-fry for another 2 minutes, or until all the vegetables are tender-crisp.

4. Combine the Noodles and Sauce:
    - Add the cooked yakisoba noodles and the cooked pork back to the skillet with the vegetables.
    - Pour the prepared sauce over the noodles and toss everything together until well coated.
    - Stir-fry for an additional 2-3 minutes, or until the noodles are heated through and evenly coated with the sauce.
5. Serve:
    - Transfer the Yakisoba Stir-Fry to serving plates or bowls.
    - Garnish with toasted sesame seeds and thinly sliced green onions, if desired.
    - Serve hot and enjoy the delicious flavors of homemade Yakisoba with pork and vegetables!

Yakisoba is a versatile dish, so feel free to customize it with your favorite vegetables and protein choices. It's a perfect meal for a quick and tasty dinner!

Taiyaki Fish-Shaped Cake with Sweet Red Bean Filling

Ingredients:

- 1 cup all-purpose flour
- 1 tablespoon cornstarch
- 1/4 teaspoon baking powder
- 2 tablespoons sugar
- 1 egg
- 3/4 cup milk
- 1/2 teaspoon vanilla extract
- Sweet red bean paste (store-bought or homemade)
- Vegetable oil or cooking spray, for greasing the Taiyaki pan

Instructions:

1. Prepare the Batter:
    - In a mixing bowl, sift together the all-purpose flour, cornstarch, baking powder, and sugar.
    - In a separate bowl, whisk together the egg, milk, and vanilla extract until well combined.
    - Gradually add the wet ingredients to the dry ingredients, stirring until you have a smooth batter with no lumps. The batter should have a similar consistency to pancake batter. If it's too thick, you can add a little more milk.
2. Preheat the Taiyaki Pan:
    - Preheat a Taiyaki pan over medium heat. If you don't have a Taiyaki pan, you can use a regular waffle iron or a fish-shaped mold.
3. Grease the Pan:
    - Lightly grease the Taiyaki pan with vegetable oil or cooking spray to prevent sticking.
4. Fill the Taiyaki Mold:
    - Pour a small amount of batter into each side of the Taiyaki mold, filling it about halfway.
    - Add a spoonful of sweet red bean paste in the center of one side of the mold, making sure to keep it away from the edges.
5. Cook the Taiyaki:
    - Close the Taiyaki mold and cook for 3-4 minutes, or until the Taiyaki is golden brown and crispy on the outside.

- Flip the Taiyaki mold halfway through cooking to ensure even browning on both sides.

6. Serve:
   - Once cooked, carefully remove the Taiyaki from the mold and transfer it to a plate.
   - Repeat the process with the remaining batter and sweet red bean paste until all Taiyaki are cooked.
   - Serve the Taiyaki warm and enjoy the delicious combination of crispy exterior and sweet red bean filling.

You can also get creative with the fillings and try other options such as chocolate, custard, or Nutella. Taiyaki is best enjoyed fresh but can be stored in an airtight container for a day or two. Enjoy your homemade Taiyaki!

Oyakodon Chicken and Egg Rice Bowl

Ingredients:

- 2 boneless, skinless chicken thighs or breasts, thinly sliced
- 1 small onion, thinly sliced
- 2-3 large eggs
- 2 tablespoons soy sauce
- 1 tablespoon mirin (sweet rice wine)
- 1 tablespoon sake (Japanese rice wine) or dry sherry
- 1 tablespoon sugar
- 1/2 cup dashi (Japanese broth) or chicken broth
- Cooked Japanese rice (short-grain or sushi rice)
- Thinly sliced green onions, for garnish
- Toasted sesame seeds, for garnish (optional)
- Shichimi togarashi (Japanese seven spice blend), for garnish (optional)

Instructions:

1. Prepare the Chicken and Onion:
    - Thinly slice the chicken thighs or breasts and the onion.
    - In a small bowl, mix together soy sauce, mirin, sake, sugar, and dashi (or chicken broth) to make the sauce.
2. Cook the Chicken and Onion:
    - Heat a skillet or frying pan over medium heat. Add a little oil if necessary.
    - Add the sliced onion to the pan and sauté until softened.
    - Add the sliced chicken to the pan and cook until no longer pink and cooked through.
3. Add the Sauce:
    - Pour the sauce mixture into the skillet with the chicken and onion.
    - Bring the mixture to a simmer and let it cook for a couple of minutes until the sauce slightly thickens.
4. Add the Beaten Eggs:
    - In a small bowl, lightly beat the eggs.
    - Slowly pour the beaten eggs over the chicken and onion mixture in the skillet.
    - Allow the eggs to set slightly around the edges.
5. Finish Cooking:

- Once the eggs are partially set, gently stir the mixture to distribute the eggs evenly.
- Continue to cook until the eggs are fully cooked but still slightly soft and custardy.

6. Serve:
   - Spoon the chicken and egg mixture over bowls of cooked Japanese rice.
   - Garnish with thinly sliced green onions, toasted sesame seeds, and a sprinkle of shichimi togarashi, if desired.
   - Serve the Oyakodon hot and enjoy the delicious combination of tender chicken, soft eggs, and flavorful sauce over rice!

Oyakodon is a comforting and satisfying dish that's perfect for a quick and easy meal at any time of the day. Enjoy its rich flavors and hearty appeal!

Zucchini and Carrot Sunomono Vinegar Salad

Ingredients:

- 1 zucchini
- 1 carrot
- 1/4 cup rice vinegar
- 2 tablespoons sugar
- 1/2 teaspoon salt
- 1 tablespoon soy sauce
- 1 tablespoon toasted sesame seeds (optional), for garnish
- Thinly sliced green onions (optional), for garnish

Instructions:

1. Prepare the Vegetables:
    - Wash the zucchini and carrot thoroughly.
    - Using a mandoline slicer or a sharp knife, thinly slice the zucchini and carrot into matchstick-like strips or very thin rounds. You can also use a julienne peeler for this step.
2. Make the Dressing:
    - In a small bowl, combine rice vinegar, sugar, salt, and soy sauce. Stir until the sugar and salt are dissolved.
3. Marinate the Vegetables:
    - Place the sliced zucchini and carrot in a large bowl.
    - Pour the dressing over the vegetables and toss gently to coat them evenly.
    - Cover the bowl and refrigerate the salad for at least 30 minutes to allow the flavors to meld and the vegetables to marinate.
4. Serve:
    - Once chilled, transfer the marinated zucchini and carrot to a serving plate or bowl.
    - Garnish with toasted sesame seeds and thinly sliced green onions, if desired.
    - Serve the Zucchini and Carrot Sunomono Vinegar Salad as a refreshing side dish or appetizer alongside your favorite Japanese meals.

This Sunomono salad is light, crisp, and bursting with flavor, making it a perfect accompaniment to a variety of dishes or a refreshing snack on its own. Enjoy its delightful combination of sweet, sour, and savory flavors!

Chicken Karaage Japanese Fried Chicken

Ingredients:

- 500g boneless, skinless chicken thighs or breasts, cut into bite-sized pieces
- 3 cloves garlic, minced
- 1 tablespoon ginger, grated
- 2 tablespoons soy sauce
- 1 tablespoon sake (Japanese rice wine) or dry sherry
- 1 tablespoon mirin (sweet rice wine)
- 1 tablespoon sesame oil
- 1/2 teaspoon salt
- 1/4 teaspoon black pepper
- 1 cup potato starch or cornstarch
- Vegetable oil, for deep-frying
- Lemon wedges, for serving (optional)
- Japanese mayonnaise, for serving (optional)
- Shichimi togarashi (Japanese seven spice blend), for serving (optional)

Instructions:

1. Marinate the Chicken:
    - In a large bowl, combine the minced garlic, grated ginger, soy sauce, sake, mirin, sesame oil, salt, and black pepper.
    - Add the chicken pieces to the marinade and toss to coat them evenly. Cover the bowl and refrigerate for at least 30 minutes, or up to 4 hours, to allow the flavors to meld.
2. Coat the Chicken:
    - Place the potato starch or cornstarch in a shallow dish or bowl.
    - Remove the marinated chicken from the refrigerator and dredge each piece in the starch, shaking off any excess.
3. Fry the Chicken:
    - Heat vegetable oil in a deep fryer or large skillet to 350°F (175°C).
    - Carefully add the coated chicken pieces to the hot oil in batches, making sure not to overcrowd the pan.
    - Fry the chicken for about 5-7 minutes, or until golden brown and cooked through, flipping them occasionally for even cooking.
    - Remove the fried chicken from the oil using a slotted spoon and drain on paper towels.

4. Serve:
   - Transfer the Chicken Karaage to a serving plate.
   - Serve hot, garnished with lemon wedges, Japanese mayonnaise, and a sprinkle of shichimi togarashi for extra flavor and spice.
   - Enjoy the crispy and flavorful Chicken Karaage as an appetizer, snack, or part of a Japanese meal!

Chicken Karaage is best enjoyed immediately while still hot and crispy. It pairs well with steamed rice, shredded cabbage, or a simple green salad.

Horenso no Goma-ae Spinach with Sesame Dressing

Ingredients:

- 1 bunch of spinach (about 200g)
- 2 tablespoons white sesame seeds
- 1 tablespoon sugar
- 1 tablespoon soy sauce
- 1 tablespoon mirin (sweet rice wine)
- 1 teaspoon sesame oil
- Pinch of salt

Instructions:

1. Prepare the Spinach:
    - Wash the spinach thoroughly under cold water to remove any dirt or debris.
    - Trim off any tough stems or thick parts of the stems.
    - Bring a pot of water to a boil. Add a pinch of salt to the water.
    - Blanch the spinach in the boiling water for about 30 seconds to 1 minute, or until wilted but still vibrant green.
    - Immediately transfer the blanched spinach to a bowl of ice water to stop the cooking process and preserve its color.
    - Once cooled, drain the spinach well and squeeze out any excess water. Use your hands or a clean kitchen towel to press out the water.
2. Prepare the Sesame Dressing:
    - In a small skillet or frying pan, toast the white sesame seeds over medium heat until golden brown and fragrant, stirring frequently to prevent burning. This should take about 2-3 minutes.
    - Transfer the toasted sesame seeds to a mortar and pestle or a spice grinder. Grind the sesame seeds until they form a coarse powder.
    - In a small bowl, combine the ground sesame seeds, sugar, soy sauce, mirin, and sesame oil. Mix well until the sugar is dissolved and the dressing is smooth.
3. Dress the Spinach:
    - Place the drained and squeezed spinach in a serving bowl.
    - Pour the sesame dressing over the spinach and toss gently to coat the leaves evenly with the dressing.
4. Serve:

- Transfer the Horenso no Goma-ae to serving plates or bowls.
- Optionally, garnish with a sprinkle of additional toasted sesame seeds for extra flavor and texture.
- Serve the spinach salad chilled or at room temperature as a refreshing and nutritious side dish.

Horenso no Goma-ae is a simple yet delicious way to enjoy spinach, showcasing its natural flavor and complementing it with the nutty aroma of sesame seeds. It's a perfect addition to any Japanese meal or a healthy snack on its own.

Red Bean Dorayaki Pancakes

Ingredients:

- 2/3 cup all-purpose flour
- 1/2 teaspoon baking powder
- 2 large eggs
- 1/4 cup granulated sugar
- 1 tablespoon honey
- 1 tablespoon water
- 1 teaspoon vanilla extract
- Sweet red bean paste (store-bought or homemade)
- Vegetable oil, for cooking

Instructions:

1. Prepare the Batter:
    - In a mixing bowl, sift together the all-purpose flour and baking powder.
    - In a separate bowl, beat the eggs and sugar together until pale and frothy.
    - Add the honey, water, and vanilla extract to the egg mixture and mix until well combined.
    - Gradually add the flour mixture to the wet ingredients, stirring until smooth and no lumps remain. The batter should have a smooth, pourable consistency.
2. Cook the Pancakes:
    - Heat a non-stick skillet or griddle over medium heat and lightly grease it with vegetable oil.
    - Pour about 1/4 cup of the batter onto the skillet to form each pancake. Cook until bubbles form on the surface of the pancake and the edges start to look set, about 2-3 minutes.
    - Carefully flip the pancakes using a spatula and cook for an additional 1-2 minutes on the other side, or until golden brown and cooked through.
    - Remove the cooked pancakes from the skillet and transfer them to a plate. Repeat the process with the remaining batter, greasing the skillet as needed between batches.
3. Assemble the Dorayaki:
    - Once the pancakes have cooled slightly, spread a spoonful of sweet red bean paste onto the center of half of the pancakes.

- Place another pancake on top of each filled pancake to form a sandwich, pressing down gently to adhere.
4. Serve:
    - Serve the Red Bean Dorayaki pancakes immediately, while still warm and soft.
    - Optionally, dust the tops of the pancakes with powdered sugar for a decorative touch.
    - Enjoy the delicious combination of fluffy pancakes and sweet red bean paste in this classic Japanese treat!

Red Bean Dorayaki is perfect for breakfast, brunch, or as a sweet snack any time of the day. Its delightful flavor and soft texture make it a favorite among both kids and adults alike.

Chicken Yakisoba Stir-Fried Noodles

Ingredients:

- 200g yakisoba noodles (or substitute with ramen noodles)
- 2 boneless, skinless chicken breasts, thinly sliced
- 1 onion, thinly sliced
- 1 carrot, julienned
- 1 bell pepper (any color), thinly sliced
- 2 cups shredded cabbage
- 2 cloves garlic, minced
- 2 tablespoons vegetable oil
- 2 tablespoons soy sauce
- 1 tablespoon oyster sauce
- 1 tablespoon Worcestershire sauce
- 1 tablespoon ketchup
- 1 teaspoon sugar
- Salt and pepper, to taste
- Toasted sesame seeds, for garnish (optional)
- Thinly sliced green onions, for garnish (optional)

Instructions:

1. Prepare the Noodles:
    - If using dried yakisoba noodles, cook them according to the package instructions until al dente. Rinse under cold water to stop the cooking process and drain well. If using fresh yakisoba noodles, follow the package instructions.
2. Cook the Chicken:
    - Heat 1 tablespoon of vegetable oil in a large skillet or wok over medium-high heat.
    - Add the sliced chicken to the skillet and cook until it is no longer pink and cooked through. Remove the chicken from the skillet and set aside.
3. Stir-Fry the Vegetables:
    - In the same skillet, add the remaining tablespoon of vegetable oil.
    - Add the minced garlic to the skillet and stir-fry for about 30 seconds, or until fragrant.
    - Add the sliced onion, julienned carrot, and sliced bell pepper to the skillet. Stir-fry for 2-3 minutes, or until the vegetables are slightly softened.

- Add the shredded cabbage to the skillet and continue to stir-fry for another 2 minutes, or until all the vegetables are tender-crisp.
4. Make the Sauce:
    - In a small bowl, combine soy sauce, oyster sauce, Worcestershire sauce, ketchup, and sugar. Mix well until the sugar is dissolved.
5. Combine Everything:
    - Add the cooked chicken back to the skillet with the vegetables.
    - Add the cooked noodles to the skillet, along with the prepared sauce.
    - Toss everything together until well combined and the noodles are evenly coated with the sauce.
    - Season with salt and pepper to taste.
6. Serve:
    - Transfer the Chicken Yakisoba to serving plates or bowls.
    - Garnish with toasted sesame seeds and thinly sliced green onions, if desired.
    - Serve hot and enjoy the delicious flavors of homemade Chicken Yakisoba!

Chicken Yakisoba is a flavorful and satisfying dish that's perfect for a quick and easy meal. It's loaded with vegetables, protein, and noodles, making it a complete and balanced dish that's sure to please everyone at the table!

Kappa Maki Cucumber Sushi Rolls

Ingredients:

- Sushi rice (prepared with rice vinegar, sugar, and salt)
- Nori sheets (seaweed)
- 1 cucumber
- Soy sauce, for serving
- Pickled ginger (gari), for serving
- Wasabi, for serving

Instructions:

1. Prepare the Sushi Rice:
    - Cook sushi rice according to package instructions.
    - In a small bowl, mix rice vinegar, sugar, and salt until dissolved. Fold this mixture into the cooked rice while it's still warm. Allow the rice to cool to room temperature.
2. Prepare the Cucumber:
    - Wash the cucumber and peel if desired. Cut it into thin, long strips, about 1/4 inch in thickness. You can remove the seeds if preferred.
3. Assemble the Sushi Rolls:
    - Place a sheet of nori on a bamboo sushi rolling mat (makisu) with the shiny side facing down.
    - Moisten your hands with water to prevent the rice from sticking. Take a handful of sushi rice and spread it evenly over the nori, leaving about half an inch of space at the top edge.
    - Arrange the cucumber strips horizontally across the center of the rice-covered nori sheet.
4. Roll the Sushi:
    - Starting from the edge closest to you, carefully roll the sushi mat away from you, enclosing the filling.
    - Apply gentle pressure to shape the sushi roll into a cylinder. Use the sushi mat to help you roll it tightly.
    - Once rolled, press gently to seal the edge of the nori.
5. Slice the Sushi Rolls:
    - Using a sharp knife, moistened with water, slice the sushi roll into individual pieces, about 1 inch thick. Wipe the knife clean between cuts to ensure clean slices.

6. Serve:
   - Arrange the Kappa Maki cucumber sushi rolls on a serving plate.
   - Serve with soy sauce, pickled ginger (gari), and wasabi on the side for dipping.
   - Enjoy the fresh and crisp flavors of Kappa Maki as a delightful appetizer or part of a sushi platter!

Kappa Maki is a simple yet delicious sushi roll that highlights the refreshing taste of cucumber. It's perfect for vegetarians or anyone who enjoys light and healthy sushi options.

Nasu Dengaku Miso-Glazed Eggplant

Ingredients:

- 2 small Japanese eggplants (or 1 large eggplant)
- 2 tablespoons white miso paste
- 1 tablespoon mirin (sweet rice wine)
- 1 tablespoon sake (Japanese rice wine)
- 1 tablespoon sugar
- 1 teaspoon soy sauce
- Vegetable oil, for brushing
- Toasted sesame seeds, for garnish
- Thinly sliced green onions, for garnish

Instructions:

1. Prepare the Eggplant:
    - Preheat your broiler or grill to medium-high heat.
    - Cut the eggplants in half lengthwise. Score the flesh of each half in a crosshatch pattern, being careful not to cut through the skin.
    - Brush the cut sides of the eggplants lightly with vegetable oil.
2. Broil or Grill the Eggplant:
    - Place the eggplant halves, cut side up, on a baking sheet if using the broiler, or directly on the grill grates if grilling.
    - Broil or grill the eggplants for about 5-7 minutes, or until they are tender and lightly charred, turning them halfway through cooking for even browning.
3. Make the Miso Glaze:
    - While the eggplants are cooking, prepare the miso glaze. In a small saucepan, combine white miso paste, mirin, sake, sugar, and soy sauce.
    - Cook the mixture over medium heat, stirring constantly, until the sugar is dissolved and the sauce is smooth and slightly thickened. Remove from heat.
4. Glaze the Eggplant:
    - Once the eggplants are cooked, remove them from the broiler or grill.
    - Brush the cut sides of each eggplant half with the miso glaze, coating them evenly.
5. Broil or Grill Again:
    - Return the glazed eggplants to the broiler or grill, cut side up.

- Broil or grill for an additional 1-2 minutes, or until the miso glaze is caramelized and bubbly.
6. Serve:
    - Transfer the Nasu Dengaku to a serving plate.
    - Garnish with toasted sesame seeds and thinly sliced green onions.
    - Serve hot as a delicious appetizer or side dish.

Nasu Dengaku is a flavorful and satisfying dish that showcases the natural sweetness of eggplant complemented by the rich umami flavors of the miso glaze. Enjoy it as part of a Japanese-inspired meal or as a standalone dish!

Chuka Kurage Sunomono Jellyfish Salad

Ingredients:

- 1 package (about 200g) of pre-cooked jellyfish (chuka kurage)
- 1 cucumber, thinly sliced
- 1/4 cup rice vinegar
- 2 tablespoons soy sauce
- 1 tablespoon sugar
- 1 teaspoon sesame oil
- Toasted sesame seeds, for garnish
- Thinly sliced green onions, for garnish

Instructions:

1. Prepare the Jellyfish:
    - If the jellyfish is packaged in salt, rinse it thoroughly under cold water to remove excess salt. If it's already cooked, simply drain it from the packaging liquid.
2. Prepare the Dressing:
    - In a small bowl, mix together rice vinegar, soy sauce, sugar, and sesame oil until the sugar is dissolved and the ingredients are well combined. This will be your dressing.
3. Marinate the Jellyfish:
    - Place the prepared jellyfish in a bowl.
    - Pour the dressing over the jellyfish and toss gently to coat. Allow the jellyfish to marinate in the dressing for at least 15-20 minutes to absorb the flavors.
4. Assemble the Salad:
    - Arrange the thinly sliced cucumbers on a serving plate.
    - Top the cucumbers with the marinated jellyfish, spreading it out evenly.
5. Garnish and Serve:
    - Sprinkle toasted sesame seeds and thinly sliced green onions over the top of the salad for garnish.
    - Serve the Chuka Kurage Sunomono chilled as an appetizer or side dish.

Chuka Kurage Sunomono is light, refreshing, and bursting with flavor, making it a perfect dish for hot summer days or as part of a Japanese meal. Enjoy its unique texture and tangy taste!

Kakiage Mixed Vegetable Tempura

Ingredients:

- Assorted vegetables (such as carrots, onions, bell peppers, sweet potatoes, zucchini, and/or mushrooms), thinly sliced
- Tempura batter mix (available at Asian grocery stores) or homemade tempura batter (see below)
- Vegetable oil, for deep-frying

For the Tempura Batter:

- 1 cup all-purpose flour
- 1 tablespoon cornstarch
- 1 cup ice-cold water
- 1 egg, beaten (optional)
- Pinch of salt

Instructions:

1. Prepare the Vegetables:
    - Wash and peel the vegetables as needed. Slice them thinly into julienne strips or rounds. It's best to keep the vegetable slices uniform in size for even cooking.
2. Make the Tempura Batter:
    - In a mixing bowl, combine the all-purpose flour, cornstarch, and a pinch of salt.
    - Gradually add the ice-cold water to the dry ingredients, stirring gently until just combined. Be careful not to overmix; lumps are okay.
    - If using, whisk in the beaten egg until incorporated into the batter.
3. Heat the Oil:
    - Heat vegetable oil in a deep fryer or large pot to 350°F (175°C). Use enough oil to fully submerge the vegetables during frying.
4. Mix the Vegetables with the Batter:
    - In a large bowl, combine the sliced vegetables with the tempura batter. Mix gently until the vegetables are evenly coated with the batter.
5. Fry the Kakiage:

- Carefully drop spoonfuls of the vegetable and batter mixture into the hot oil, making sure not to overcrowd the fryer. You may need to fry in batches.
- Fry the kakiage for 2-3 minutes, or until golden brown and crispy, turning them occasionally for even cooking.
- Remove the fried kakiage from the oil using a slotted spoon and drain on paper towels to remove excess oil.

6. Serve:
    - Transfer the Kakiage Mixed Vegetable Tempura to a serving plate.
    - Serve hot as an appetizer or side dish, with dipping sauce such as tentsuyu (tempura dipping sauce) or tempura sauce mixed with grated daikon radish.
    - Enjoy the crispy and delicious Kakiage alongside your favorite Japanese dishes!

Kakiage Mixed Vegetable Tempura is a delightful and versatile dish that's perfect for enjoying the natural flavors and textures of a variety of vegetables. Experiment with different vegetable combinations and enjoy the crispy goodness of homemade tempura!

Inarizushi Fried Tofu Pouch Sushi

Ingredients:

- 1 package of aburaage (fried tofu pouches)
- 2 cups sushi rice (short-grain Japanese rice)
- 2 cups water (for cooking rice)
- 1/4 cup rice vinegar
- 2 tablespoons sugar
- 1 teaspoon salt
- Optional fillings for the pouches: cooked carrots, cooked shiitake mushrooms, cooked green beans, or sesame seeds

Instructions:

1. Prepare the Sushi Rice:
    - Rinse the sushi rice under cold water until the water runs clear. This removes excess starch.
    - Cook the rinsed rice with 2 cups of water in a rice cooker or on the stovetop according to the package instructions.
    - While the rice is cooking, mix the rice vinegar, sugar, and salt in a small saucepan. Heat gently until the sugar and salt are dissolved. Set aside to cool.
2. Prepare the Aburaage:
    - Open the package of aburaage and carefully remove each tofu pouch.
    - Place the aburaage in a bowl of hot water for a few minutes to remove excess oil and soften them. Then gently squeeze out any excess water.
    - Cut each aburaage pouch in half horizontally to create pockets for the rice.
3. Stuff the Aburaage Pouches:
    - Once the aburaage pouches are cool enough to handle, gently open each one and stuff it with a spoonful of sushi rice. Be careful not to overfill.
    - Optionally, you can add cooked carrots, shiitake mushrooms, green beans, or sesame seeds to the rice before stuffing the pouches.
4. Close the Pouches:
    - Fold the sides of the aburaage over the rice to enclose it completely. Press gently to seal the edges.
5. Serve:
    - Arrange the stuffed Inarizushi on a serving plate.

- Serve at room temperature or chilled, garnished with sesame seeds or thinly sliced nori strips if desired.

Inarizushi is a delightful and portable sushi option that's perfect for picnics, bento boxes, or as part of a sushi platter. Enjoy its sweet and savory flavors with your favorite Japanese condiments like soy sauce, wasabi, and pickled ginger!

Sake Steamed Clams with Sake and Butter

Ingredients:

- 1 kg fresh clams (such as Manila or littleneck clams)
- 1/2 cup sake (Japanese rice wine)
- 4 tablespoons unsalted butter
- 2 cloves garlic, minced
- 2 tablespoons chopped fresh parsley (for garnish)
- Freshly ground black pepper, to taste
- Crusty bread, for serving (optional)

Instructions:

1. Prepare the Clams:
    - Rinse the clams under cold water, scrubbing them lightly to remove any sand or debris. Discard any clams with broken shells or that do not close when tapped.
2. Cook the Clams:
    - In a large pot or Dutch oven, melt the butter over medium heat.
    - Add the minced garlic to the pot and sauté for about 1 minute until fragrant.
    - Pour in the sake and bring it to a simmer.
3. Steam the Clams:
    - Add the cleaned clams to the pot and cover with a lid.
    - Steam the clams for about 5-7 minutes, shaking the pot occasionally, until the clams have opened. Discard any clams that do not open after cooking.
4. Finish the Dish:
    - Once the clams have opened, remove the pot from the heat.
    - Using a slotted spoon, transfer the cooked clams to serving bowls, leaving the cooking liquid in the pot.
    - Season the cooking liquid with freshly ground black pepper to taste.
5. Serve:
    - Pour the sake and butter sauce over the steamed clams in the serving bowls.
    - Garnish with chopped fresh parsley for a burst of color and flavor.
    - Serve immediately, accompanied by crusty bread for soaking up the delicious sauce.

Sake steamed clams with sake and butter are best enjoyed fresh and hot, straight from the pot. This dish is perfect as an appetizer or main course, and it pairs wonderfully with a glass of chilled sake. Enjoy the exquisite flavors of the sea with this elegant and comforting Japanese dish!

Edamame Boiled Soybeans with Sea Salt

Ingredients:

- 1 pound (about 450g) fresh or frozen edamame (unshelled soybeans)
- Sea salt, to taste

Instructions:

1. Prepare the Edamame:
    - If using frozen edamame, thaw them according to the package instructions. If using fresh edamame, rinse them under cold water.
2. Boil the Edamame:
    - Fill a large pot with water and bring it to a boil over high heat.
    - Once the water is boiling, add the edamame to the pot.
    - Cook the edamame for about 3-5 minutes, or until they are tender and heated through. The cooking time may vary depending on whether you are using fresh or frozen edamame.
3. Drain and Season:
    - Once the edamame are cooked, drain them in a colander.
    - Transfer the cooked edamame to a serving bowl or platter.
4. Season with Sea Salt:
    - Sprinkle the boiled edamame generously with sea salt, to taste.
    - Toss the edamame gently to ensure that they are evenly coated with the salt.
5. Serve:
    - Serve the edamame immediately, while they are still warm.
    - Optionally, you can provide additional sea salt on the side for those who prefer a saltier flavor.

Edamame boiled soybeans with sea salt are typically served as an appetizer or snack, either on their own or alongside other Japanese dishes. They are delicious, nutritious, and fun to eat, making them a popular choice for gatherings and parties. Enjoy the simple pleasure of popping open the pods and savoring the tender, flavorful beans inside!

Chicken Nanban Fried Chicken with Tartar Sauce

Ingredients:

For the Chicken:

- 4 boneless, skinless chicken breasts or thighs
- Salt and pepper, to taste
- All-purpose flour, for dredging
- 2 eggs, beaten
- Panko breadcrumbs, for coating
- Vegetable oil, for frying

For the Nanban Sauce:

- 1/4 cup soy sauce
- 1/4 cup rice vinegar
- 2 tablespoons sugar
- 2 tablespoons mirin
- 1 tablespoon sake
- 1 teaspoon grated ginger
- 1 teaspoon grated garlic
- 1 green onion, thinly sliced (for garnish)
- 1 tablespoon sesame seeds (for garnish)

For the Tartar Sauce:

- 1/2 cup mayonnaise
- 2 tablespoons finely chopped pickles or pickle relish
- 1 tablespoon lemon juice
- 1 teaspoon Dijon mustard
- Salt and pepper, to taste

Instructions:

1. Prepare the Tartar Sauce:

- In a small bowl, mix together mayonnaise, chopped pickles or relish, lemon juice, and Dijon mustard until well combined.
- Season with salt and pepper to taste. Refrigerate until ready to serve.

2. Prepare the Nanban Sauce:

- In a small saucepan, combine soy sauce, rice vinegar, sugar, mirin, sake, grated ginger, and grated garlic.
- Heat the mixture over medium heat, stirring occasionally, until the sugar is dissolved and the sauce has slightly thickened. Remove from heat and set aside.

3. Prepare the Chicken:

- Season the chicken breasts or thighs with salt and pepper.
- Dredge each piece of chicken in flour, shaking off any excess.
- Dip the chicken into the beaten eggs, then coat them thoroughly with panko breadcrumbs.
- Heat vegetable oil in a large skillet or deep fryer to 350°F (175°C).
- Fry the chicken pieces in batches for about 5-6 minutes per side, or until golden brown and cooked through. Drain on paper towels.

4. Finish the Chicken Nanban:

- Once all the chicken is fried, cut each piece into bite-sized strips.
- Dip the fried chicken pieces into the Nanban sauce, coating them evenly.
- Arrange the chicken on a serving platter and drizzle with any remaining Nanban sauce.
- Garnish with thinly sliced green onions and sesame seeds.

5. Serve:

- Serve the Chicken Nanban hot, with tartar sauce on the side for dipping.
- Enjoy the crispy fried chicken with the tangy and sweet Nanban sauce, complemented by the creamy tartar sauce.

Chicken Nanban with tartar sauce is a delicious and satisfying dish that's perfect for lunch or dinner. Serve it with steamed rice and a side of salad for a complete meal.

Enjoy the unique flavors of this Japanese comfort food!

www.ingramcontent.com/pod-product-compliance
Lightning Source LLC
LaVergne TN
LVHW081606060526
838201LV00054B/2102